Learn the way to **Rearrange** *the* **Deranged**

JUMBLED SENTENCES & PARAGRAPHS

SC GUPTA
B.Sc, MA, M.Com, LLB, DLL, CAIIB

KUMKUM GUPTA
MA

✳arihant
ARIHANT PUBLICATIONS (INDIA) LIMITED

ARIHANT PUBLICATIONS (INDIA) LIMITED

꣚ Administrative & Production Offices

Regd. Office

'Ramchhaya' 4577/15, Agarwal Road, Darya Ganj, New Delhi -110002
Tele: 011- 47630600, 43518550

꣚ Head Office

Kalindi, TP Nagar, Meerut (UP) - 250002, Tel: 0121-7156203, 7156204

꣚ Sales & Support Offices

Agra, Ahmedabad, Bengaluru, Bareilly, Chennai, Delhi, Guwahati, Hyderabad, Jaipur, Jhansi, Kolkata, Lucknow, Nagpur & Pune.

꣚ **ISBN**   978-93-26191-22-7

꣚ **PRICE**   ₹80.00

PO No : TXT-XX-XXXXXXX-X-XX

Published by Arihant Publications (India) Ltd.

For further information about the books published by Arihant, log on to www.arihantbooks.com or e-mail at info@arihantbooks.com

Follow us on   

PREFACE

A new revised book related to 'Rearrangement of Jumbled Sentences and Paragraphs' is in front of you. In almost every Competitive Examinations in 'General English' Section, 5 to 20 questions are asked on 'Arrangement of Sentences'. Candidates are required to find the proper sequence of the given sentences. Generally, there are three types of questions based on 'Arrangement'. This book explains the proper technique of solving such questions. But it must be kept in mind that to understand any methodology or technique, candidate must be well-versed with grammatical rules and proper usage of English structure and concepts alongwith exceptions to various rules.

This book contains lots of practice exercises which will provide enough practice for any Competitive Examination. You must remember 'The more you practice, the more proficient you become' to secure good marks.

The salient features of the book are as follow:

i.   Short theory about the topic with examples for each types of 'Arrangement'.

ii. Coverage of all three types of format of 'Arrangements of Sentences' asked in various Competitive Examination.

iii. The three types include Rearrangement of Sentences (PQRS) (Type I). Rearrangement of Paragraphs (Type II) and Para-Jumbles (Type III). All three types contain practice exercises with 10 questions in each exercise alongwith questions asked in various Competitive Exams such as CDS, NDA, SSC CGL (Others), CAT, MAT, Bank (PO) & Bank (Clerk) are given.

The requirements of the candidate have been a major factor kept in mind during compilation of this book. We are sure that the book will serve the purpose of leading the reader to success.

With best wishes

Authors
129, South-West Block,
Near Eidgah, Alwar, Rajasthan
Tel - 0144-2700438, 2345714

CONTENTS

What is Sentence Arrangement?

Sentence Arrangement is about arranging a group of jumbled words in a meaningful sentence. It can also consist of a group of sentences from a paragraph which are given in the jumbled form. The candidate has to arrange them (Sentences) into a coherent paragraph.

The questions on sentence arrangement can be broadly classified into three categories :

(a) Rearrangement of Sentences   (b) Rearrangement of Paragraphs

(c) Para-jumbles

Type I   Rearrangement of Sentences

In these type of questions, a number of phrases (Usually 4) which are labelled as (P), (Q), (R), (S) etc are given. These phrases are part of a complete sentence, but are given in a jumbled order in the exam. The candidate has to re-arrange the jumbled phrases and make a meaningful sentence. The answer to these questions is given as a sequence of labels like SPQR, PSRQ etc. The candidate has to select the correct sequence out of the given options.

Targeted Exams These type of questions are asked in competitive examinations like NDA and CDS Exam.

Tips for Attempting these Questions

1. If the hint or starting part of the sentence is given try to build the remaining part of the sentence by arranging the phrases.

2. If there is no hint then read all phrases/parts of the sentence and try to get a close idea regarding the underlying sense of the sentence.

3. The first part of the sentence needs to be located first. Usually, a part that contains the main verb is the first part.

4. Once the first part of the sentence is located, you need to look at the options that are left.

5. Read the remaining options and try to figure out their correct order. Hence, you get the desired answer.

Type II Rearrangement of Paragraphs

In these type of questions, the first and last sentence of a paragraph is given. The rest of the sentences are jumbled and labelled as (P), (Q), (R), (S) etc.

The candidate has to re-arrange the jumbled sentences in order to make a coherent and meaningful paragraph. The answer to these questions is given as a series of labels such as RQPS, SQRP etc. The candidate has to select the option which has the correct sequence of labels.

Targeted Exams These type of questions are generally asked in Staff Selection Commission (SSC) examination for entry to various cadres. Apart from this, they may also be asked in NDA, CDS and MAT entrance exams.

Tips for Attempting these Questions

1. As first and last sentence of the paragraph is given, these type of questions are relatively easier to solve.
2. The first sentence hints the main topic/theme of the paragraph.
3. We need to find out a sentence (Second sentence) that has the linkage of the event after the first sentence.
4. The rest of the sentences can be found out in sequence.
5. These sentences would be connected so as to make sense with the last sentence (Which is given).

Type III Para-Jumbles

In this type, four or six sentences marked A, B, C, D, E, F etc are given in a jumbled form. The candidate is required to arrange these sentences in a proper order.

When properly sequenced, these sentences form a coherent and meaningful paragraph. These types of questions can be asked in a different way as well. The candidate can be asked a few questions with respect to the correct order of sentences in the paragraph.

Targeted Exams These type of questions are generally asked in Bank PO & Clerks, IDBI, CAT, MAT and SSC etc.

Tips for Attempting these Questions

1. Try to understand the passage, if you can make out the meaning behind the passage, you will definitely get the correct order.
2. Create a pair of two sentences, i.e. if 6 sentences, then create 3 pairs each having 2 sentences.
3. Try to find out clues while making a pair, most of the time there are some connecting words that form a bridge between two sentences.
4. Once you have identified the pairs, all you need to do is to re-order these pairs to form meaningful passage.
5. Try to find out the pair that looks independent and place it as introduction, the pair that looks like a result as last.
6. Go through the arrangement and check the logical meaning of the paragraph and see if it conveys a meaningful flow. If you think the sequence lacks logic, re-arrange again till you start seeing some logic.

Practice Exercises

Type I Rearrangement of Sentences

Direction *In the following items, some parts of sentence have been jumbled up, you are required to rearrange these parts which are labelled as P, Q, R and S to produce the correct sentence. Choose correct sequence and mark in your answer sheet.*

Exercise 1

1. About half of
   the blindness of(P)/ vitamin A shortage(Q)/ is attributed to(R)/ children in India (S)
   The correct sequence should be
   (a) QRPS   (b) RPSQ
   (c) PSRQ   (d) SPQR   *[CDS, 2012]*

2. It was reported that
   the table(P)/ belonging to a lady(Q)/ with three carved legs(R)/ was sold the next day by auction(S)
   The correct sequence should be
   (a) PRQS   (b) QPRS
   (c) PQSR   (d) PQRS   *[CDS, 2012]*

3. The wings
   are so small(P)/ useless for flying(Q)/ of some birds(R)/ that they are(S)
   The correct sequence should be
   (a) RPSQ   (b) QSPR
   (c) PRSQ   (d) SRPQ   *[CDS, 2011]*

4. The person
   at night(P)/ next door(Q)/ sings loudly(R)/ who lives(S)
   The correct sequence should be
   (a) PRQS   (b) QSRP
   (c) SQRP   (d) PQSR   *[CDS, 2011]*

5. We have
   to provide(P)/ both people and ecosystems(Q)/ the ability(R)/ with the water they need(S)

The correct sequence should be

(a) RPQS   (b) QRPS

(c) SRPQ   (d) RSPQ   *[CDS, 2011]*

6. Physical training

   the character of(P)/ who are going to be responsible citizens(Q)/ can shape well(R)/ young boys and girls(S)

   The correct sequence should be

   (a) RPSQ   (b) QSPR

   (c) RSPQ   (d) QPSR   *[CDS, 2008]*

7. I was

   to see a mongoose(P)/ just in time(Q)/ with an egg in its mouth(R)/ scurrying across the grass(S)

   The correct sequence should be

   (a) SRQP   (b) QPSR

   (c) SPQR   (d) QRSP   *[CDS, 2008]*

8. After having got up from bed

   the Magistrate(P)/ to bring coffee(Q)/ ordered the attendant(R)/ immediately(S)

   The correct sequence should be

   (a) PQRS   (b) SPQR

   (c) SPRQ   (d) PRQS   *[NDA & NA, 2012]*

9. You should better

   of getting a good response(P)/ so that(Q)/ we will be sure(R)/ work hard(S)

   The correct sequence should be

   (a) RSQP   (b) SQRP

   (c) SQPR   (d) RPQS   *[NDA & NA, 2012]*

10. You'll

    know how to do it (P)/ have to (Q)/ because she does not(R)/ help her(S)

    The correct sequence should be

    (a) QSPR   (b) SRPQ

    (c) QPRS   (d) QSRP   *[NDA & NA, 2013]*

<h1 align="center">Exercise 2</h1>

1. It must not be imagined
that a walking tour,(P)/ is merely a better or worse way(Q)/as some
would say(R)/ of seeing the country(S)
The correct sequence should be
(a) RPQS   (b) PRQS
(c) PQSR   (d) PQRS   *[CDS, 2012]*

2. It
in the news bulletin(P)/ did not feature (Q)/ that this matter(R)/
was surprising(S)
The correct sequence should be
(a) PSQR   (b) RQPS
(c) QSPR   (d) SRQP   *[CDS, 2012]*

3. You won't believe me,
to see him(P)/ I went(Q)/ but whenever(R)/ he was out(S)
The correct sequence should be
(a) PQRS   (b) QRSP
(c) SRPQ   (d) RQPS   *[CDS, 2011]*

4. As the car
stood up(P)/ to greet him(Q)/ came near the door(R)/ the
waiters(S)
The correct sequence should be
(a) QPSR   (b) SRPQ
(c) RSPQ   (d) PRSQ   *[CDS, 2011]*

5. At last
had come(P)/ she had been(Q)/ the moment(R)/ waiting for(S)
The correct sequence should be
(a) RQSP   (b) QSPR
(c) SQRP   (d) QRPS   *[CDS, 2011]*

6. A tortoise
fly in the air(P)/ two geese(Q)/ everyday(R)/ watched(S)
The correct sequence should be
(a) SQPR   (b) RSQP
(c) PSQR   (d) RPSQ   *[CDS, 2008]*

7. Every experience in life makes
   on some of the cells(P)/ or other nerve centres(Q)/ of the brain(R)/
   an impression(S)
   The correct sequence should be

   (a) SPRQ   (b) QRSP

   (c) RSPQ   (d) PSQR   *[NDA & NA, 2013]*

8. His uncle
   after he joined(P)/ did not send(Q)/ the college(R)/ money for his
   expenses(S)
   The correct sequence should be

   (a) QRSP   (b) RSQP

   (c) QSPR   (d) SRPQ   *[NDA & NA, 2011]*

9. We are doing
   to the people(P)/ to give relief(Q)/ all we can(R)/ but more funds
   are needed(S)
   The correct sequence should be

   (a) PQRS   (b) RQPS

   (c) QPRS   (d) SPQR   *[NDA & NA, 2010]*

10. The boy
    in the competition(P)/ who was wearing spectacles(Q)/ won many
    prizes(R)/ held in our college(S)
    The correct sequence should be

    (a) PQRS   (b) RPSQ

    (c) QRPS   (d) QPSR   *[NDA & NA, 2010]*

Exercise 3

1. Seventy-two people
   reports PTI(P)/ were affected by food poisoning(Q)/ including
   several women and children(R)/ of the central part of the city(S)
   The correct sequence should be

   (a) SPQR   (b) PQRS

   (c) RSPQ   (d) RSQP   *[CDS, 2014]*

2. If you buy the economy pack
   the manufacturers, wanting to promote the sales(P)/ which is quite
   cheap(Q)/ have devised a number of schemes(R)/and to ensure
   clearance of stocks(S)

The correct sequence should be
(a) QPSR   (b) PQRS
(c) RSQP   (d) QRSP   *[CDS, 2011]*

3. For a moment
that I am terribly old(P)/ since I was child(Q)/ and that it is very
long time ago (R)/ I forget(S)
The correct sequence should be
(a) QPRS   (b) PSRQ
(c) RPQS   (d) SPRQ   *[CDS, 2009]*

4. Climate
cultures and political structures(P)/ in that it affects the entire(Q)/
change is a truly unifying phenomenon(R)/ world irrespective of
national borders(S)
The correct sequence should be
(a) RSQP   (b) PQSR
(c) RQSP   (d) PSQR   *[CDS, 2008]*

5. Many of
but plants and that we do not(P)/ eat meat since that amounts to
harming animals(Q)/ us humans pride ourselves(R)/ by declaring
that we eat nothing(S)
The correct sequence should be
(a) RQSP   (b) PSQR
(c) RSPQ   (d) PQSR   *[CDS, 2008]*

6. How strange that a refugee
should fall in love(P)/ when he had got to America(Q)/with a girl
less than half his age(R)/ who had by the skin of his teeth escaped
death in Germany(S)
The correct sequence should be
(a) RQPS   (b) SPRQ
(c) RPQS   (d) SQPR   *[CDS, 2008]*

7. We are proud that
as our chief guest(P)/ our Mayor(Q)/ is a former student of this
college(R)/ who is presiding over today's function(S)
The correct sequence should be
(a) PQRS   (b) QPSR
(c) PQSR   (d) QSPR   *[NDA & NA, 2012]*

8. At the end of the morning exercise,
   the soldiers(P)/ to get ready to leave(Q)/ were asked(R)/ for an unknown destination(S)
   The correct sequence should be
   (a) PQRS   (b) RSPQ
   (c) SRQP   (d) PRQS   *[NDA & NA, 2012]*

9. For fear
   that may or may not affect them perhaps at first (P)/ of upsetting young people(Q)/ only healthy people over 80 should be sequenced(R)/ about their genetic propensities(S)
   The correct sequence should be
   (a) SQPR   (b) QSRP
   (c) SQRP   (d) QSPR   *[NDA & NA, 2008]*

10. It's
    someone who's grieving but(P)/ natural to feel uncomfortable(Q)/ don't let that prevent you from being there(R)/ or awkward when you have to help(S)
    The correct sequence should be
    (a) QPSR   (b) RSPQ
    (c) QSPR   (d) RPSQ   *[NDA & NA, 2008]*

Exercise 4

1. However, noble their ends appear
   since they make (P)/ use of violence(Q)/ are bound to end up(R)/ all their acts with untold misery for all(S)
   The correct sequence should be
   (a) PQRS   (b) RQSP
   (c) SRPQ   (d) RQPS   *[CDS, 2013]*

2. Most of Hitchcock's films
   were critically acclaimed on both sides of the Atlantic(P)/ earning him both fame and fortune(Q)/ and made good money at the box office(R)/ in no small measure(S)
   The correct sequence should be
   (a) PRQS   (b) PRSQ
   (c) QPRS   (d) QSPR   *[CDS, 2012]*

3. The second test of good government is that
to every man and woman(P)/ and act only with their consent(Q)/ it
should give a log of freedom(R)/ and should treat their personalities
with respect and sympathy(S)
The correct sequence should be
(a) QSPR
(b) SRQP
(c) RPSQ
(d) PQRS
[CDS, 2010]

4. When he was a child
passed his happiest hours(P)/ the boy who was to become Britain's
Baron Haden(Q)/ staring out of his apartment window(R)/ living in
New York(S)
The correct sequence should be
(a) QSPR
(b) PRQS
(c) SQPR
(d) RSQP
[CDS, 2010]

5. It is difficult
from major news channels without a deep sense(P)/ or experience
the images and comments(Q)/ not just of fear for the future, but of
shame and embarrassment (R)/ today to pick up a newspaper(S)
The correct sequence should be
(a) QSPR
(b) SQRP
(c) QSRP
(d) SQPR
[CDS, 2008]

6. The teacher
and the pupils continued likewise with their repetition(P)/ read the
sentence again(Q)/ the pupils knew the sentence by heart(R)/
until the teacher thought(S)
The correct sequence should be
(a) PQSR
(b) PSRQ
(c) QPSR
(d) QSRP
[NDA & NA, 2011]

7. In the Middle Ages,
there was little progress(P)/ either intellectual or social(Q)/ with the
result that(R)/ teaching became the exclusive prerogative of the
church(S)
The correct sequence should be
(a) PQRS
(b) SRPQ
(c) PRSQ
(d) QPRS
[NDA & NA, 2011]

8. While traditional
   under made-up Americans aliases pretending familiarity with a
   culture and climate(P)/ India sleeps, a dynamic young cohort of
   highly skilled articulate professionals(Q)/ they've never actually
   experienced earning salaries that were undreamt of by their
   elders(R)/ works through the night in the call centres functioning
   on US time(S)   **[NDA & NA, 2008]**
   The correct sequence should be
   (a) PRQS   (b) QSPR
   (c) PSQR   (d) QRPS

9. IITs are
   of great self-confidence and competitive advantage for India
   today(P)/ in Science and Technology which has become a
   source(Q)/ as they epitomise his creation of an infrastructure for
   excellence(R)/ perhaps Jawaharlal Nehru's most consequential
   legacy(S)   **[NDA & NA, 2008]**
   The correct sequence should be
   (a) QPSR   (b) SRQP
   (c) QRSP   (d) SPQR

10. A diversified use
    as a heating or power generation fuel by converting gas into(P)/
    adding a new dimension to the traditional use of gas(Q)/ of natural
    gas is emerging(R)/ amongst other products, high quality diesel
    transportation fuel virtually free of sulphur(S)
    The correct sequence should be
    (a) RPQS   (b) SQPR
    (c) RQPS   (d) SPQR   **[NDA & NA, 2007]**

Exercise 5

1. When the rain stopped
   we set out(P)/ to stay the night(Q)/ where we had planned(R)/ for
   next town(S)
   The correct sequence should be
   (a) PQRS   (b) QPRS
   (c) PRQS   (d) PSRQ   **[CDS, 2012]**

2. I felt

like a Cold War spy(P)/ for a moment(Q)/ to whom a critical secret (R)/ had just been revealed(S)

The correct sequence should be

(a) PQRS   (b) PSQR

(c) PRSQ   (d) QPRS   *[CDS, 2012]*

3. What a wonderful thing it is

the Sun is the source(P)/ of all-power(Q)/ in some way or the other (R)/ to think that (S)

The correct sequence should be

(a) SRPQ   (b) PSQR

(c) SQRP   (d) PQSR   *[CDS, 2012]*

4. The dacoit

many heinous crimes(P)/ had committed(Q)/ who carried a reward of fifty thousand rupees(R)/ on his head(S)

The correct sequence should be

(a) PRSQ   (b) QPSR

(c) RQPS   (d) RSQP   *[CDS, 2012]*

5. Although, the train was delayed by half an hour

he could not reach the station(P)/ to catch the train(Q)/ in time (R)/ bound for Delhi(S)

The correct sequence should be

(a) PQRS   (b) PRQS

(c) QRPS   (d) PSQR   *[CDS, 2012]*

6. Dr Ravi

has been appointed reader in the University(P)/ in the recent selections(Q)/ in a Private Degree College(R)/ who was working as a lecturer(S)

The correct sequence should be

(a) PQSR   (b) SRPQ

(c) QPSR   (d) SQRP   *[CDS, 2012]*

7. It was true that

the pet dog(P)/ would never sleep anywhere(Q)/ we once had(R)/ except on sofa(S)

The correct sequence should be

(a) PQRS   (b) SPQR

(c) RPQS   (d) PRQS   *[CDS, 2013]*

8. One should remember that lying at the side of the road(P)/ if we found our neighbour(Q)/ unable to move because of a broken leg(R)/ we should show our neighbourliness(S)

The correct sequence should be

(a) SQPR   (b) PQRS
(c) QRPS   (d) SQRP   *[CDS, 2012]*

9. It is believed that

the tiger(P)/ Mr Saxena(Q)/ being severely injured in the first encounter(R)/ was too terrified to make a second attempt at shooting(S)

The correct sequence should be

(a) RPSQ   (b) PRSQ
(c) RQSP   (d) PSQR   *[CDS, 2012]*

10. The clerk

on the desk(P)/ left the money(Q)/ in the safe(R)/ which he should have locked up(S)

The correct sequence should be

(a) PQRS   (b) RSPQ
(c) QPRS   (d) QPSR   *[CDS, 2014]*

Exercise 6

1. The principal has issued a notice

will have to vacate the hostel(P)/ that those junior doctors(Q)/ if they fail to join duty by Monday next(R)/ who are participating in the strike(S)

The correct sequence should be

(a) QSPR   (b) RQSP
(c) PRQS   (d) QRSP   *[CDS, 2012]*

2. I have read

who by some mysterious laws of her nature(P)/ in the form of a foul and poisonous snake(Q)/ the story of a fairy(R)/ was condemned to appear in certain seasons(S)

The correct sequence should be

(a) QRSP   (b) PQRQ
(c) RQPS   (d) RPSQ   *[CDS, 2012]*

3. All religions are

to advance the cause of peace (P)/in a holy partnership (Q)/justice and freedom (R)/bound together (S)

The correct sequence should be

(a) PQRS   (b) PRQS

(c) SPQR   (d) SQPR   *[CDS, 2013]*

4. It is

for a man (P)/when he accompanies a lady (Q)/an accepted custom (R)/to open the door (S)

The correct sequence should be

(a) PSQR   (b) RPSQ

(c) PSRQ   (d) PQRS   *[CDS, 2013]*

5. One monsoon evening

the farmer returned from the fields(P)/ when the sky was overcast with threatening clouds(Q)/ and found a group of children playing on the road(R)/ a little earlier than usual(S)

The correct sequence should be

(a) QSPR   (b) QPSR

(c) QRSP   (d) PQRS   *[CDS, 2012]*

6. The fire

before any serious damage was done (P)/by volunteers (Q)/was controlled (R)/in the godown (S)

The correct sequence should be

(a) SRQP   (b) RSPQ

(c) RQPS   (d) QRSP   *[CDS, 2013]*

7. When John saw

coming head on (P)/towards him (Q)/a speeding truck (R)/he ran for life (S)

The correct sequence should be

(a) RPQS   (b) RSPQ

(c) PRSQ   (d) PQRS   *[CDS, 2013]*

8. They decided

for their friends (P)/that afternoon (Q)/to buy some presents (R)/to go shopping (S)

The correct sequence should be

(a) QRSP   (b) SQRP

(c) QRPS   (d) PQSR   *[CDS, 2013]*

9. Whenever I see the model

who started it (P)/is the face of the man (Q)/of our factory (R)/what comes to my mind (S)

The correct sequence should be

(a) SRQP   (b) RSQP

(c) QPRS   (d) PQRS   **[NDA & NA, 2011]**

10. All religions are

to advance the cause of peace (P)/in a holy partnership (Q)/justice and freedom (R)/bound together (S)

The correct sequence should be

(a) PRQS   (b) PQRS

(c) SQPR   (d) SPQR   **[CDS, 2014]**

Exercise 7

1. William Shakespeare

in his lifetime (P)/the great English dramatist (Q)/wrote thirty-five plays (R)/and several poems (S)

The correct sequence should be

(a) PQRS   (b) RSPQ

(c) QSRP   (d) QRSP   **[NDA & NA, 2010]**

2. Fame

by showing off (P)/to the best advantage (Q)/one's ability and virtue (R)/is earned (S)

The correct sequence should be

(a) PQRS   (b) SPRQ

(c) PRSQ   (d) PQSR   **[CDS, 2010]**

3. Movies made in

all around the globe (P)/Hollywood in America (Q)/by people (R)/are seen at the same time (S)

The correct sequence should be

(a) QSRP   (b) QRPS

(c) PSRQ   (d) QPSR   **[CDS, 2010]**

4. The natives of Caribbean

regarded the papaya (P)/because of its ability (Q)/as a magic tree (R)/to keep them healthy (S)

The correct sequence should be

(a) PRSQ   (b) PRQS

(c) RPQS   (d) RPSQ   **[CDS, 2013]**

5. Some educationists

   should not be exposed to (P)/believe that (Q)/young children (R)/too much television viewing (S)

   The correct sequence should be

   (a) RSPQ   (b) QPRS

   (c) QRPS   (d) PQRS   *[CDS, 2013]*

6. The doctor told

   the patient (P)/to give an injection to (Q)/the nurse (R)/after four hours (S)

   The correct sequence should be

   (a) RQPS   (b) RPSQ

   (c) QPSR   (d) PSRQ   *[CDS, 2011]*

7. The Judge

   lied to the court (P)/why he had (Q)/asked the accused (R)/inspite of his oath (S)

   The correct sequence should be

   (a) PSRQ   (b) QPSR

   (c) PRQS   (d) RQPS   *[CDS, 2011]*

8. His father said

   and stop (P)/on trivial things (Q)/wasting your time (R)/now get up (S)

   The correct sequence should be

   (a) SPRQ   (b) PSRQ

   (c) QRSP   (d) RQSP   *[CDS, 2011]*

9. The stranger's movements

   and the police (P)/him (Q)/arrested (R)/aroused suspicion (S)

   The correct sequence should be

   (a) SQPR   (b) RQPS

   (c) SPRQ   (d) RPQS   *[CDS, 2011]*

10. The future

    is glommy (P)/outlook (Q)/animal (R)/of the noble (S)

    The correct sequence should be

    (a) PQSR   (b) QPSR

    (c) RPSQ   (d) QSRP   *[CDS, 2011]*

Exercise 8

1. When he knew

he sat down under a tree (P)/about what to do next (Q)/and thought for a long time (R)/that there was no more hope (S)

The correct sequence should be

(a) SRQP   (b) SPRQ

(c) QPSR   (d) RSPQ   *[CDS, 2013]*

2. He wanted

to reach his place of work (P)/ who used to travel 20 miles (Q)/to buy a scooter (R)/for his son (S)

The correct sequence should be

(a) PQRS   (b) QRSP

(c) QSRP   (d) RSQP   *[CDS, 2013]*

3. They went out

in the morning by a bus (P)/ to spend the day at Bhimli, (Q)/a famous picnic spot, (R)/some 25 km away (S)

The correct sequence should be

(a) PQRS   (b) QRSP

(c) RSPQ   (d) SRQP   *[CDS, 2013]*

4. After the awarding speeches

the prizes given (P)/and (Q)/had been delivered (R)/I got up to address the gathering (S)

The correct sequence should be

(a) SRQP   (b) SPQR

(c) RSQP   (d) RQPS   *[CDS, 2013]*

5. It is

to be admitted (P)/not necessary that (Q)/to an engineering college (R)/you qualify an entrance examination (S)

The correct sequence should be

(a) SRQP   (b) QSPR

(c) QRPS   (d) SRPQ   *[NDA & NA, 2013]*

6. My little sister

in school (P)/instead of reading books (Q)/who was quite intelligent (R)/played with dolls (S)

The correct sequence should be

(a) PRSQ   (b) RSPQ

(c) QPSR   (d) PRQS   *[NDA & NA, 2012]*

7. Our educationalists are
to teach children (P)/too often anxious (Q)/without any utility (R)/
so many languages (S)
The correct sequence should be
(a) PQRS   (b) QRSP
(c) SRQP   (d) QPSR   **[NDA & NA, 2011]**

8. A scientist has shown that,
when anyone holds (P)/a burning cigarette (Q)/near their leaves
(R)/plants react with fear (S)
The correct sequence should be
(a) PQRS   (b) QRSP
(c) SPQR   (d) PQSR   **[NDA & NA, 2011]**

9. Language is
to the other person (P)/communicating (Q)/only a means of
(R)/one's thoughts and emotions (S)
The correct sequence should be
(a) PQSR   (b) RQSP
(c) QRSP   (d) SPQR   **(NDA & NA, 2011)**

10. The Prime Minister declared that
those states (P)/will get all help and aid (Q)/where family planning
(R)/is effected very efficiently (S)
The correct sequence should be
(a) PRSQ   (b) PQRS
(c) RSPQ   (d) QPSR   **[CDS, 2014]**

Exercise 9

1. He said that
two years before (P)/and that he could produce (Q)/he had passed
his examination (R)/his certificate (S)
The correct sequence should be
(a) SPQR   (b) QSRP
(c) RPQS   (d) PRSQ   **[CDS, 2013]**

2. For dropping kilos,
it is safe to cut your fat intake (P)/and maintaining weight loss
(Q)/to 20% of your calories (R)/even further (S)
The correct sequence should be
(a) PRQS   (b) QSPR
(c) SPRQ   (d) QPRS   **[NDA & NA, 2011]**

3. Although, the motion
   until it had been considerably amended (P)/from the House
   (Q)/received general support (R)/it was not carried (S)
   The correct sequence should be
   (a) PQRS   (b) SQPR
   (c) RQSP   (d) QRSP   *[CDS, 2011]*

4. What greater thing is there
   for two human souls to feel (P)/to rest on each other in all sorrow (Q)/
   that they are joined for life (R)/to strengthen each other in all labour (S)
   The correct sequence should be
   (a) SQRP   (b) RPQS
   (c) QRSP   (d) PRSQ   *[CDS, 2010]*

5. Just as the goodness of movies
   like the things which they represent, (P)/does not consist in being
   (Q)/so the goodness of music does not consist (R)/in its being like
   the noises we know (S)
   The correct sequence should be
   (a) QPRS   (b) PQRS
   (c) RPSQ   (d) SPRQ   *[CDS, 2013]*

6. All the students
   affirmed positively that (P)/responded eagerly to the question and
   (Q)/the political affiliation of student unions interviewed on
   television (R)/ was undesirable(S)
   The correct sequence should be
   (a) PQRS   (b) SRPQ
   (c) RPQS   (d) SQPR   *[CDS, 2011]*

7. It is foolish
   of those who posses them (P)/to believe that (Q)/will result in
   victory (R)/the use of nuclear weapons (S)
   The correct sequence should be
   (a) RSPQ   (b) QSRP
   (c) PRQS   (d) SQPR   *[CDS, 2010]*

8. A distressing fact is that
   social accountability (P)/ are dominated only by greed (Q)/many
   people today (R)/and there is hardly any (S)
   The correct sequence should be
   (a) SRPQ   (b) QSRP
   (c) PRQS   (d) RQSP   *[CDS, 2010]*

9. I once had

every morning (P)/a client who swore (Q)/for the past four years (R)/she had a headache (S)

The correct sequence should be

(a) PRSQ   (b) QSPR

(c) RPQS   (d) SQRP   *[CDS, 2010]*

10. People know

not only of the smokers themselves (P)/that smoking tobacco (Q)/but also of their companions (R)/is injurious to the health (S)

The correct sequence should be

(a) PSQR   (b) RPSQ

(c) QPRS   (d) QSPR   *[CDS, 2011]*

Exercise 10

1. Recently,

containing memorable letters of Churchill (P)/a book (Q)/has been published (R)/by a reputed publisher (S)

The correct sequence should be

(a) QRPS   (b) QPRS

(c) PQRS   (d) RPQS   *[CDS, 2013]*

2. As the situation has changed,

since we last discussed this matter (P)/it was best to contact you (Q)/it appeared to me (R)/without losing time (S)

The correct sequence should be

(a) PQRS   (b) PRSQ

(c) PRQS   (d) SPRQ   *[CDS, 2013]*

3. The Indian woman wants

in a male dominated society (P)/as an equal partner (Q)/and it is not too much to demand (R)/her rightful place (S)

The correct sequence should be

(a) SRPQ   (b) RSQP

(c) SQPR   (d) QPSR   *[CDS, 2013]*

4. This is a letter

by a young lady (P)/who was lately wounded in a duel (Q)/written passionately (R)/wherein she laments the misfortune of a gentleman (S)

The correct sequence should be

(a) SRPQ   (b) RSQP

(c) RPSQ   (d) QPSR   *[CDS, 2013]*

5. Hardly had my brother descended from the plane
   when the people (P)/waved and cheered (Q)/who had come to receive him (R)/from the lounge (S)
   The correct sequence should be
   (a) PRQS   (b) PQRS
   (c) SPQR   (d) PRSQ   *[CDS, 2014]*

6. My friend
   when he was going to his office (P)/met with an accident (Q)/on his scooter (R)/due to rash driving (S)
   The correct sequence should be
   (a) PQRS   (b) PRQS
   (c) SRQP   (d) QSRP   *[CDS, 2014]*

7. Mohan, the son of my friend,
   gave me a set of pens (P)/which is very precious (Q)/while working in Japan (R)/who died in an accident (S)
   The correct sequence should be
   (a) PQRS   (b) SRPQ
   (c) RSPQ   (d) SPQR   *[CDS, 2014]*

8. The boy said,
   I am not going to the school (P)/with my friends in the classroom (Q)/where my teacher scolds me (R)/when I want to play (S)
   The correct sequence should be
   (a) PQRS   (b) PSQR
   (c) SQPR   (d) PRSQ   *[CDS, 2014]*

9. Mr Saxena was a profound scholar who
   was held in high esteem by all those (P)/who read his books and visited him regularly (Q)/till his untimely death (R)/though not popular with the general public (S)
   The correct sequence should be
   (a) PQRS   (b) RPQS
   (c) SRQP   (d) SPQR   *[CDS, 2010]*

10. The government wants that
    by the veterinary surgeons (P)/by the butchers (Q)/all the goats slaughtered (R)/must be medically examined (S)
    The correct sequence should be
    (a) RPSQ   (b) QSRP
    (c) RQSP   (d) PRSQ   *[CDS, 2010]*

Answers

Exercise 1

1. (c) **2.** (a) **3.** (a) **4.** (c) **5.** (a) **6.** (a) **7.** (b) **8.** (d) **9.** (b) **10.** (d)

Exercise 2

1. (b) **2.** (d) **3.** (d) **4.** (c) **5.** (a) **6.** (a) **7.** (a) **8.** (c) **9.** (b) **10.** (c)

Exercise 3

1. (d) **2.** (a) **3.** (d) **4.** (c) **5.** (c) **6.** (b) **7.** (d) **8.** (d) **9.** (d) **10.** (c)

Exercise 4

1. (c) **2.** (a) **3.** (c) **4.** (c) **5.** (d) **6.** (c) **7.** (b) **8.** (b) **9.** (b) **10.** (c)

Exercise 5

1. (d) **2.** (d) **3.** (a) **4.** (d) **5.** (b) **6.** (b) **7.** (d) **8.** (c) **9.** (c) **10.** (d)

Exercise 6

1. (a) **2.** (d) **3.** (d) **4.** (b) **5.** (b) **6.** (c) **7.** (a) **8.** (b) **9.** (b) **10.** (c)

Exercise 7

1. (d) **2.** (b) **3.** (a) **4.** (b) **5.** (c) **6.** (a) **7.** (d) **8.** (a) **9.** (c) **10.** (d)

Exercise 8

1. (b) **2.** (d) **3.** (a) **4.** (d) **5.** (b) **6.** (b) **7.** (d) **8.** (c) **9.** (b) **10.** (a)

Exercise 9

1. (c) **2.** (b) **3.** (c) **4.** (d) **5.** (a) **6.** (d) **7.** (b) **8.** (d) **9.** (b) **10.** (d)

Exercise 10

1. (b) **2.** (c) **3.** (c) **4.** (c) **5.** (a) **6.** (b) **7.** (b) **8.** (d) **9.** (d) **10.** (c)

Type II Rearrangement of a Jumbled Paragraphs

Direction *In these questions, the first and the last sentences of the paragraph are given and numbered as S_1 and S_6. The rest of the passage is split into four parts and named P, Q, R and S. These four parts are jumbled. Read the sentences and find out, which of the four combinations is correct. Then find the correct answer.*

Exercise 1

1. S_1 : Nick was bored with life.
   P : He caught the same bus to work.
   Q : He did the same things in office.
   R : He got up exactly at the same time.
   S : Every day was exactly the same.
   S_6 : He came home at the same time.
   The correct sequence should be
   (a) QPRS   (b) PSRQ
   (c) SQRP   (d) SRPQ   *[SSC Steno, 2014]*

2. S_1 : If we look around us today
   P : that is shattered by violence,
   Q : the effects of which
   R : a world
   S : we will find
   S_6 : continue to influence us.
   The correct sequence should be
   (a) RSPQ   (b) RPQS
   (c) SRPQ   (d) QPSR   *[SSC Steno, 2014]*

3. S_1 : When the Impressionists   P : they made them look like
   Q : everyday and often putting   R : people you would see
   S : painted pictures of people S_6 : more emphasis on the scene
   The correct sequence should be
   (a) PRQS   (b) SPRQ
   (c) RQPS   (d) SRQP   *[SSC LDC, 2013]*

4. S_1 : Sherlock Holmes is the
   P : who is in a state of grace
   Q : is raised to the status
   R : because in him scientific curiosity
   S : exceptional individual
   S_6 : of a heroic passion.
   The correct sequence should be
   (a) SPRQ   (b) RPSQ
   (c) PRQS   (d) SRQP   *[SSC LDC, 2013]*

5. S_1 : The goals of our present system
   P : schooling is to prepare
   Q : students for the examination system
   R : which will take them to the
   S : of primary and secondary
   S_6 : best technical institutions in the country.
   The correct sequence should be
   (a) PRQS   (b) PSQR
   (c) SPQR   (d) QPRS   *[SSC LDC, 2013]*

6. S_1 : The Leeds University   P : a number
   Q : offers   R : to international
   S : of scholarships S_6 : students.
   The correct sequence should be
   (a) QPSR   (b) PQRS
   (c) QRPS   (d) RPSQ   *[SSC Steno, 2012]*

7. S_1 : The World Health Organisation
   P : the greatest villain   Q : has pointed out
   R : is   S : that tobacco
   S_6 : in the history of humankind.
   The correct sequence should be
   (a) QPRS   (b) RPSQ
   (c) QSRP   (d) PQRS   *[SSC Steno, 2012]*

8. S_1 : My friend's protest   P : a cry
   Q : turned out to be   R : injustice
   S : against S_6 : in the wilderness.
   The correct sequence should be
   (a) QRSP   (b) RQSP
   (c) PRQS   (d) SRQP   *[SSC Steno, 2012]*

9. S_1 : There is   P : as the gift

    Q : and love for humanity   R : no such thing

    S : of brotherhood S_6 : in this world.

    The correct sequence should be

    (a) QPRS   (b) RSPQ

    (c) RPSQ   (d) PRSQ   *[SSC Steno, 2012]*

10. S_1 : Academicians

    P : who have been involved in the debate

    Q : including former Vice-Chancellors

    R : that the legislation can help providing a uniform character

    S : on a common university law, think

    S_6 : to the university bodies such as senate, syndicate etc.

    The correct sequence should be

    (a) PSRQ   (b) QPSR

    (c) RQPS   (d) SRQP   *[SSC Steno, 2012]*

Exercise 2

1. S_1 : The role of modern youth

    P : as they have to not only

    Q : than that of their forefathers

    R : keep the torch of freedom aloft

    S : is far more challenging

    S_6 : but also keep it always lit.

    The correct sequence should be

    (a) SRPQ   (b) RSPQ

    (c) SQPR   (d) PRSQ   *[SSC CGL, 2012]*

2. S_1 : Modern education is bookish

    P : the harsh realities of life.

    Q : imparted in schools and colleges

    R : and divorced from

    S : The so called liberal education

    S_6 : Does not help students earn their livelihood.

    The correct sequence should be

    (a) RPSQ   (b) PRSQ

    (c) RPQS   (d) QSPR   *[SSC CGL, 2012]*

3. S_1 : The Great Lakes are a group of

    P : Superior is so called not because it is the largest

    Q : on the border between the USA and Canada.

    R : Five freshwater lakes in North America

    S : but because it is higher upstream than the others.

    S_6 : Huron takes its name from the name French settlers gave it.

The correct sequence should be

(a) SPRQ   (b) QPSR

(c) PRQS   (d) RQPS   *[SSC CGL, 2012]*

4. S_1 : Youths are the assets and hope of a nation.

    P : in making India a great

    Q : steeped in old cultural values

    R : They can play a vital role

    S : democratic, progressive and prosperous country

    S_6 : but equipped with modern scientific look.

The correct sequence should be

(a) RPSQ   (b) QPRS

(c) SPRQ   (d) PRSQ   *[SSC CGL, 2012]*

5. S_1 : Porcelain became popular at the beginning of the 19th century.

    P : in a kiln at more than 2372 degrees Fahrenheit.

    Q : refer to both China and Bisque dolls.

    R : Porcelain is made by firing special clays

    S : Porcelain is used generically to

    S_6 : Only a few types of clays can withstand such high temperatures.

The correct sequence should be

(a) RPQS   (b) SQRP

(c) PSQR   (d) QRSP   *[SSC CGL, 2012]*

6. S_1 : Human behaviours are regulated by their

    P : a person's working pattern as well as living style.

    Q : between these selves has an adverse effect upon

    R : Work done is the self-portrait

    S : real self and social self. Conflict

    S_6 : of the person who did it.

The correct sequence should be

(a) QRSP   (b) PQRS

(c) RPQS   (d) SQPR   *[SSC CGL, 2012]*

7. S_1 : The Australians were very proud and felt privileged
   P : in their country
   Q : to host the Olympics-2000
   R : as it elevated their stature
   S : in the eyes of the world
   S_6 : at the threshold of the new millennium.
   The correct sequence should be
   (a) QPRS   (b) PRQS
   (c) SPQR   (d) RQSP   *[SSC CGL, 2012]*

8. S_1 : Ram has an important examination to sit for in a few weeks time.
   P : but he could not concentrate .
   Q : what he saw was not very nice he was very pale.
   R : He sat down to prepare for it
   S : After a while he looked at himself in the mirror
   S_1 : He said to himself, "What I need is fresh air".
   The correct sequence should be
   (a) PQRS   (b) RPSQ
   (c) QSPR   (d) SQRP   *[SSC CGL, 2012]*

9. S_1 : Once there was a king,
   P : On the next day a group of merchants passed on that way.
   Q : The people in his kingdom were very lazy.
   R : The king wanted to teach them a lesson.
   S : One night he had arranged a big stone in the middle of the road.
   S_6 : They didn't move the stone, but passed round it.
   The correct sequence should be
   (a) SQPR   (b) RPQS
   (c) QRSP   (d) QSRP   *[SSC Steno, 2011]*

10. S_1 : Poliomyelitis or polio is a serious infection.
   P : It often attacks children paralysing them for life.
   Q : In the 1950's a vaccine against the disease was introduced.
   R : Hence, it is sometimes called infantile paralysis.
   S : It is caused by a virus.
   S_6 : Since then polio has been eliminated to a great extent.
   The correct sequence should be
   (a) PSRQ   (b) SPQR
   (c) SPRQ   (d) PRQS   *[SSC Steno, 2011]*

Exercise 3

1. S_1 : Although, fruits can no longer grow once picked,

 P : taking in oxygen and

 Q : they continue to respire for sometime,

 R : giving off carbon dioxide,

 S : just as human beings do

 S_6 : when they breathe.

The correct sequence should be

(a) QPRS   (b) SQPR

(c) RPQS   (d) PRSQ   *[SSC CGL, 2011]*

2. S_1 : The vegetable bin of my refrigerator contained an assortment of weird-looking items.

 P : The carrots dropped into U shapes as I picked them up with the tips of my fingers.

 Q : To the right of the oranges was a bunch of carrots that had begun to sprout points, spikes and tendrils.

 R : Near the carrots was a net bag of onions.

 S : Next to a shriveled, white-coated lemon were two oranges covered with blue fuzz.

 S_6 : Each onion had sent curling shoots through the net until the whole thing resembled a mass of green spaghetti.

The correct sequence should be

(a) SQPR   (b) QSRP

(c) PRSQ   (d) RSQP   *[SSC CGL, 2011]*

3. S_1 : There was no proper light system on the highway.

 P : In addition, clouds were gathering in the sky.

 Q : The night was darker than usual.

 R : Then suddenly, the wind dropped,

 S : The atmosphere now was very stuffy.

 S_6 : The Moon also hid behind the clouds and it made the night gloomier.

The correct sequence should be

(a) QRPS   (b) RPQS

(c) QPRS   (d) SPRQ   *[SSC CGL, 2011]*

4. S_1 : AIDS is a disease caused by a virus called HIV.

P : This results in the victim's inability to defend themselves from any infections leading to death.

Q : This disease destroys part of the body's immune system.

R : AIDS patients are carriers of the virus.

S : People who are infected develop AIDS within five to ten years.

S_6 : And they are infected for years without knowing it and transmit the disease to others.

The correct sequence should be

(a) QPSR   (b) PSQR

(c) RSQP   (d) SRPQ   *[SSC CGL, 2011]*

5. S_1 : Helen Keller has an ageless quality about her in keeping with her amazing life story.

P : Although warned by this human reaction, she has no wish to be set aside from the rest of mankind.

Q : She is an inspiration to both blind and who can see everywhere.

R : When she visited Japan after World War II, boys and girls from remote villages ran to her, crying 'Helen Keller'.

S : Blind, deaf and mute from early childhood, she rose above her triple handicap to become one of the best known characters in the modern world.

S_6 : She believes the blind should live and work with their fellows, with full responsibility.

The correct sequence should be

(a) QPSR   (b) PQSR

(c) RSQP   (d) SQRP   *[SSC CGL, 2011]*

6. S_1 : India led the battle of freedom against imperialism.

P : That technique brought us success.

Q : We therefore championed the cause of other countries.

R : We fought it with a special technique.

S : We are happy that they achieved freedom.

S_6 : But some countries are still slaves.

The correct sequence should be

(a) QSRP   (b) SRPQ

(c) RPQS   (d) RSQP   *[SSC CGL, 2011]*

7. S_1 : A lot of people simply dump their rubbish in open bins.

P : All sorts of diseases are carried by the flies.

Q : Then they come into the house and infect uncovered food.

R : In this rubbish, the flies breed and multiply.

S : Such carelessness invites flies to the rubbish.

S_6 : Consumption of such food can only bring disease and sickness.

The correct sequence should be

(a) SPQR

(b) RQPS

(c) RPQS

(d) SRQP   *[SSC CPO, 2011]*

8. S_1 : Six years old Prabodh aimed his toy gun at his sister while playing.

P : "You may aim at the pole or at the wall or at the tree, where no one can get hurt."

Q : Mother got up immediately saying, "No one shoots a human being" and calmly removed the gun from Prabodh.

R : Still Prabodh aimed his gun at the kid.

S : When his mother saw this she said, "No, Prabodh! Not at the baby!"

S_6 : With such a firm action on his mother's part, Prabodh realised where the gun should not be aimed.

The correct sequence should be

(a) PRSQ

(b) QSPR

(c) SPRQ

(d) SRQP   *[SSC CPO, 2011]*

9. S_1 : A man wearing dark sunglasses walked into the bank.

P : Then he shouted, "Give me all your money, all the money in this bank right now."

Q : Everyone in the lobby screamed and started running.

R : He went up to the teller and held up a hand grenade for all to see.

S : Nervously the young female teller handed the man three big bags loaded with cash.

S_6 : Holding the grenade in one hand and the bags on the other, he walked out of the building.

The correct sequence should be

(a) PSRQ

(b) QSPR

(c) RPQS

(d) SRQP   *[SSC CPO, 2011]*

10. S_1 : Snakes are the most feared of all reptiles.

P : Superstition and ignorance prevents proper treatment.

Q : It is also beneficial to man.

R : Snake is not a source of fear and harm.

S : Many people are killed by snakes in India and all over the world.
S_6 : Medicines are made from its poison.
The correct sequence should be
(a) PRSQ   (b) QRSP
(c) SPRQ   (d) SRQP   *[SSC CPO, 2011]*

Exercise 4

1. S_1 : Education in India had a glorious beginning.

    P : But after the British rule, it faced many changes.

    Q : It went on for centuries with the same glory.

    R : English as the medium of instruction had a very great response.

    S : One of the changes was the introduction of English as the medium of instruction.

    S_6 : As the Britishers left we had a complexity of opinions regarding English.

The correct sequence should be
(a) PQRS   (b) QPSR
(c) PQSR   (d) SRPQ   *[SSC CGL, 2010]*

2. S_1 : It is the responsibility of parents to teach the young moral values in life.

    P : Many children take advantage of their parents busy schedule.

    Q : This results in children's ignorance of social values.

    R : The reason behind it is that parents are quite busy now-a-days.

    S : Now-a-days parents spend very meagre time with children.

    S_6 : As such, the society is going away from the value system.

The correct sequence should be
(a) SRPQ   (b) PQRS
(c) SQRP   (d) SPQR   *[SSC CGL, 2010]*

3. S_1 : A rocket burns a fuel that makes a great deal of gas at the back of the rocket.

    P : Ordinary fuel will burn only in air, because it needs the oxygen in the air.

    Q : A rocket can therefore travel outside the atmosphere in space where there is no air.

    R : This gas pushes against the rocket and sends it forward

    S : However, rocket fuels have their oxygen in them and so they burn without air.

S_6 : In fact, it will travel faster in space than in the air because the friction of the air is not there to slow it down.

The correct sequence should be

(a) QSRP (b) RPSQ

(c) SQPR (d) PRQS *[SSC SI, 2010]*

4. S_1 : Some of the other patrons are even more of a problem than the theatre itself.

P : They make noises and create disturbances at their seats.

Q : Some act as if they were at home in their own living room watching the TV set.

R : People are often messy, so that you're constantly aware of all the food they're eating

S : Many people in the theatre often show themselves to be inconsiderate.

S_6 : People are also always moving around near you, creating a disturbance and interrupting your enjoyment the movie.

The correct sequence should be

(a) SPQR (b) PSRQ

(c) QRSP (d) RSQP *[SSC SI, 2010]*

5. S_1 : A friend's rudeness is much more damaging than a stranger's.

P : you feel hurt instead of being angry.

Q : you feel that you're being taken for granted.

R : When a friend says sharply, "I don't have time to talk to you just now,"

S : When a friend shows up late for lunch or a shopping trip, with no good reason,

S_6 : Friends after all, are supposed to make up for the thoughtless cruelties of strangers.

The correct sequence should be

(a) RPSQ (b) PRSQ

(c) SPQR (d) QSPR *[SSC SI, 2010]*

6. S_1 : Einstein was a bad student.

P : He attended classes regularly and took down careful notes.

Q : His friend Marcel Grossman, on the other hand, was an irreproachable student.

R : These notes were shared with Einstein.

S : He resented having to attend lectures.

S_6 : If Einstein passed his examinations, it was only because of Grossman.

The correct sequence should be

(a) SQPR   (b) QRPS

(c) PSRQ   (d) RSQP   **[SSC TA, 2008]**

7. S_1 : Creating and modifying a school time table is a complex task.

P : 'TT Plus' closely models the real world time table creation tasks.

Q : So is the job of computerising it.

R : All time tables can be viewed on the screen before they are actually printed.

S : It has a comprehensive manual and useful glossary of terms.

S_6 : It relieves you of the anxiety to get it all right.

The correct sequence should be

(a) QPSR   (b) RPSQ

(c) SPRQ   (d) PQSR   **[SSC TA, 2008]**

8. S_1 : When she got to her house, there was nothing to retrieve.

P : All valuable were smashed or stolen.

Q : The curtains were burned; books were ripped to shreds.

R : Her medals and trophies had been flung everywhere.

S : The house had been completely ransacked.

S_6 : Mrs M stood in the centre of her bedroom looking at a ruined copy of the Holy book, forcing back her tears.

The correct sequence should be

(a) PQRS   (b) PRQS

(c) SPRQ   (d) RSQP   **[SSC SO, 2007]**

9. S_1 : We do not know whether the machines are the masters or we are.

P : They must be given or rather 'fed' with coal and given petrol to drink from time to time.

Q : Already man spends most of his time looking after and waiting upon them.

R : Yet we have grown so dependent on them that they have almost become the masters now.

S : It is very true that they were made for the sole purpose of being man's servants.

S_6 : And if they don't get their meals when they expected them, they will just refuse to work.

The correct sequence should be

(a) RSQP (b) RSPQ

(c) SPQR (d) SRQP *[SSC SO, 2007]*

10. S_1 : Freedom is first of all a personal matter.

P : A man who will not submit to the discipline of his chosen occupation is not free to be a great surgeon, engineer, golfer and executive.

Q : Life imposes a drastic discipline on all living things, including human beings.

R : We are free to eat poison or jump off a tall building, but not to escape the consequences.

S : We are bound by the laws of cause and effect.

S_6 : Nature, morever, binds the arbitrary limits of mind and body; we are not free to do, by whatever effort, what is beyond our capacity.

The correct sequence should be

(a) QRSP (b) RSPQ

(c) PQRS (d) SRQP *[SSC SO, 2007]*

Exercise 5

1. S_1 : The man who does his duty without any selfish desire for fruit may be called a sanyasi as well as yogi.

P : The man who has achieved much evenness of temper will be serene, because his mere thoughts are changed with the strength of action.

Q : He would practise yoga, i.e. evenness of temper and cannot, but perform action.

R : The root of the matter is that one should not allow his mind to flit from one object of desire to another and from that to a third.

S : But he who abstains from action altogether is only an idler.

S_6 : A yogi is one who is not attached to his objects of sense or to action and whose mind has ceased to roam restlessly.

The correct sequence should be

(a) SRQP (b) RQPS

(c) QRSP (d) PRSQ *[SSC CGL, 2010]*

2. S_1 : The teacher training agency in England hopes to make teaching one of the top three professions.

   P : They have also demanded that the campaign should be matched by improved pay scales, work load and moral so as to avoid recruitment problems with an aim to raise the image of the teaching profession.

   Q : A series of advertisements are now being screened showing famous people speaking about teachers they remember and admire.

   R : An amount of $ 100 million has been set aside to combat the shortage of applicants for teacher training.

   S : Teacher Unions have welcomed this campaign.

   S_6 : It is high time for the Indian Government also to think on similar lines and take steps to lift up the sinking morale of the teaching profession.

   The correct sequence should be

   (a) QRPS   (b) RPSQ

   (c) RQSP   (d) QPSR   *[SSC CGL, 2010]*

3. S_1 : This is a company that prides itself on its carefully matured extensive distribution blocks and mentor network.

   P : The company also plans a foray into the service sector by setting up a chain of launderettes across the country.

   Q : Yet today, pre-cooked chapattis and readymade mixes are a big market.

   R : And that's not all.

   S : Today, the idea may appear a trifle ambitious, but remember that it was not so long ago that the same things were said about the market for ready-to-eat foods and branded cereals.

   S_6 : Disposable incomes are rising in the metros and big cities and time is at a premium.

   The correct sequence should be

   (a) RPSQ   (b) PSQR

   (c) PQRS   (d) RPQS   *[MAT, 2009]*

4. S_1: The woman who lives a normal life is able to check the swelling conceit and egotism of her menfolk simply because her outlook is so different

   S_6 : and both ranges of interest make her what only fools deny her to be, namely, essentially practical, her eye is steadily fixed on the concrete thing and she mistrusts that chasing of the wild goose, which is one of the chief pastimes and delights of man.

P : she is primarily concerned with little ordinary things, the minutiae of talk and behaviour e.g. on the one hand and with very big ones, the colossal elementary facts of life, such as birth, mating and death on the other

Q : the first are personal and particular, whereas the second, those enormous facts about life which women are never allowed to lose sight of, are, of course, universal, meaning just as much in the Fiji Islands as they do here

R : her interest are at once narrower and wider than those of men

S : it is more personal and yet more impersonal

The correct sequence should be

(a) PQSR   (b) PRSQ

(c) SPQR   (d) SRPQ   [CDS, 2014]

5. S_1 : What soda-water is composed of you may see for yourself if you watch your glass as it stands on the table after you have slaked your first thirst

S_6 : 'carbonic acid' is the old name for it, but it is more correct to name it, when it is out of the water, 'carbon dioxide'.

P : the liquid is plain water, as you will find out if you are too slow about drinking

Q : you will see that it is separating into two different things, a liquid and a gas

R : the gas is so heavy that you can fairly drink it from the glass and it has, as you know, a tingle-tangle taste

S : the other is a heavy, sour and invisible gas that slips up through the water in little bubbles and collects in the empty half of the glass

The correct sequence should be

(a) QRSP   (b) PRQS

(c) QPSR   (d) RSPQ   [CDS, 2014]

6. S_1 : If you want to film a scene in slow motion you run the camera twice as fast as usual, which sounds ridiculous but isn't

S_6 : on the screen, everything appears at half the speed at which the camera recorded it when it was filmed.

P : if you are filming in slow motion, however, the camera runs at twice the normal speed, yet, inspite of this, the projector which shows the film will be run at the normal speed and this means that the projecter will show the film at half the speed at which it was photographed

Q : this is because the camera which took the pictures and the projector which shows them run at the same speed

R : when a film camera is running at normal speed, it takes twenty-four pictures a second

S : when the film is run through the film-projector in the camera twenty-four pictures a second appear on the screen

The correct sequence should be

(a) PSRQ   (b) PSQR

(c) SRQP   (d) RSQP   **[CDS, 2014]**

7. S_1 : Ronald Ross was born in Almora, in the Himalayas in 1857

S_6 : Manson directed him to an effective study of the disease and with his help, Ross solved the mystery in three years.

P : he began to feel that he ought to try to do something about it

Q : he was educated in England and returned to India as an officer in the Indian Medical Service

R : he started to study malaria and during a vacation to England, met Patrick Manson and studied tropical diseases under him

S : his medical conscience was stirred by the appalling disease and misery with which he was surrounded in the course of his work

The correct sequence should be

(a) SRPQ   (b) QRSP

(c) PQRS   (d) RPSQ   **[CDS, 2013]**

8. S_1 : Human ways of life have steadily changed.

S_6 : during the last few years change has been even more rapid than usual.

P : from that time to this, civilisation has always been changing

Q : About ten thousand years ago, man lived entirely by hunting

R : ancient Egypt-Greece, the Roman empire, the dark ages and the middle ages, the renaissance, the age of modern science and of modern nations, one has succeeded the other and history has never stood still.

S : a settled civilised life began only when agriculture was discount

The correct sequence should be

(a) QSRP   (b) QSPR

(c) RSQP   (d) SPRQ   **[CDS, 2013]**

9. S_1 : Solar hot water system that can supply hot water at an approximate temperature of 60°C continuously, have recently been introduced

S_6 : larger quantities of water can be heated by increasing the number of solar collectors.

P : a similar 200 litre system, but with two collectors, ideal for a family of five or six would cost around ₹ 7250

Q : a 100 litre per day system, suitable for a family of two or three, would cost around ₹ 4270

R : these rates, however, do not include the plumbing acquired to connect the system to the kitchen, bathroom or toilet of the building, transportation, installation and taxes

S : this includes the price of solar collector, a 100 litre insulated storage tank with fittings and an automatic water heater to be used during the monsoons or in an emergency.

The correct sequence should be

(a) RPQS   (b) QSPR

(c) SRQP   (d) QPSR   *[NDA & NA, 2009]*

10. S_1 : I last visited Kandy almost 10 years ago

S_6 : set around low, forested hills, with the Mahavelli river flowing nearby, the landscape has an instance yet tranquil beauty.

P : the bomb blasts and ugly face of ethnic conflict have not robbed the place of its gracious pace of life

Q : the artificial lake, which dominates the landscape of the city, was built by its last king in 1806

R : located in central Sri Lanka, at an elevation of about 1600 ft, Kandy was the last Sinhala out post of autonomy, resisting both Portuguese and Dutch rule before it succumbed to the British in 1818

S : most famous for its temple of the tooth, a golden pagoda housing a sacred relic of the Buddha, Kandy is a gentle, elegant and imperturbable city

The correct sequence should be

(a) RPQS   (b) SPRQ

(c) QPSR   (d) PSQR   *[NDA & NA, 2009]*

Exercise 6

1. S_1 : Rohan steered the jeep

    P : the path to which was muddy and bumpy,

    Q : making it a difficult drive and

    R : down the muddy road to the camp site

    S : he discovered after a few miles

    S_6: that it was the wrong road.

    The correct sequence should be

    (a) RPQS   (b) SQPR

    (c) QRPS   (d) PRSQ   **[SSC CGL, 2012]**

2. S_1 : If he changes his mind,

    P : and he will not commit

    Q : Joe has learned his lesson,

    R : the same mistake again,

    S : we shall know for sure that

    S_6 : but only time will tell.

    The correct sequence should be

    (a) RPQS   (b) SQPR

    (c) QRPS   (d) PRSQ   **[SSC CGL, 2012]**

3. S_1 : A number of linguists

    P : of languages spoken by

    Q : the world's five billion people

    R : contend that all of the thousands

    S : can be traced back to a common root language

    S_6 : and have a common origin.

    The correct sequence should be

    (a) RPQS   (b) SQPR

    (c) QRPS   (d) PRSQ   **[SSC CGL, 2012]**

4. S_1 : New industries   P : interests, usually

    Q : supported by foreign   R : to their employees at all

    S : offer better salaries. S_6 : levels of responsibility.

    The correct sequence should be

    (a) PSRQ   (b) SRQP

    (c) PQRS   (d) QPSR   **[SSC CGL, 2012]**

5. S_1 : As heart disease continues

   P : increasingly interested in identifying the

   Q : to be the number one killer

   R : researchers have become

   S : in the United States

   S_6 : potential risk factors that trigger heart attack.

   The correct sequence should be

   (a) SPRQ   (b) QSRP

   (c) PRSQ   (d) RQSP   *[SSC CGL, 2012]*

6. S_1 : India is a democratic country

   P : at the hands of our representatives

   Q : but frequent elections

   R : who play political games

   S : make it a mockery

   S_6 : at the cost of the nation.

   The correct sequence should be

   (a) PRSQ   (b) SRPQ

   (c) PSRQ   (d) QSPR   *[SSC CGL, 2012]*

7. S_1 : Both plants and animals

   P : changes in form, structure, growth habits

   Q : in becoming adapted to different climatic

   R : of many sorts show remarkable

   S : and even mode of reproduction

   S_6 : environment, types of food supply or mode of living.

   The correct sequence should be

   (a) SRPQ   (b) QPRS

   (c) PRSQ   (d) RPSQ   *[SSC CGL, 2012]*

8. S_1 : Those clouds promise rain

   P : before we get caught in a flash flood

   Q : or else we will never be able to find our way home

   R : we should hurry

   S : and would be stuck here

   S_6 : for a considerable period of time.

   The correct sequence should be

   (a) RPQS   (b) SQPR

   (c) QRPS   (d) PRSQ   *[SSC CGL, 2012]*

9. S_1 : The body can never stop.

   S_6 : It comes from food.

   P : To support this endless activity, the body needs all the fuel for action.

   Q : Sometimes, it is more active than at other times, but it is always moving.

   R : Even in the deepest sleep we must breathe.

   S : The fuel must come from somewhere.

   The correct sequence should be

   (a) PQRS   (b) PRQS

   (c) QRPS   (d) SRQP   *[NDA & NA, 2015]*

10. S_1 : Hope springs eternally in the heart of man.

    S_6 : This is the central idea of the poem.

    P : But hope is everlasting.

    Q : Love, friendship and youth perish.

    R : It is nursed by the glorious elements of nature.

    S : Man derives hope from nature in his gallant struggle after some noble ideal.

    The correct sequence should be

    (a) QPRS   (b) SRQP

    (c) RSQP   (d) QPSR   *[NDA & NA, 2015]*

Exercise 7

1. S_1 : The Bermuda Triangle is an area

   P : of many unexplained disappearances,

   Q : the three points of the triangle being Miami,

   R : is famous for being the supposed site

   S : of the Atlantic Ocean off the coast of Florida and

   S_6 : Bermuda and San Juan in Puerto Rico.

   The correct sequence should be

   (a) PQRS   (b) SRPQ

   (c) QSRP   (d) RPQS   *[SSC CGL, 2011]*

2. S_1 : What is the life, full of care,

   P : No time to stand beneath the boughs

   Q : We have no time to stand and stare.

   R : No time to see, when woods we pass

S : And stare as long as sheep or cows

S_6 : Where squirrels hide their nuts in grass.

The correct sequence should be

(a) QPSR   (b) QSPR

(c) RSPQ   (d) SPRQ   *[SSC CPO, 2011]*

3. S_1 : The bee has no sense of proportion.

    P : It goes about collecting honey

    Q : It has never learnt to spend

    R : As though starvation was staring it at its face.

    S : Even with stocks sufficient for 20 generations.

    S_6 : And that is how God has made them.

    The correct sequence should be

    (a) PRQS   (b) RSQP

    (c) QSPR   (d) QRPS   *[SSC CPO, 2011]*

4. S_1 : Nalanda became India's famous centre of education.

    P : Ten thousand Buddhist monks used to live there.

    Q : It is situated near the town of Bihar Sharif.

    R : The ruins of Nalanda can still be seen.

    S : It was visited by the Chinese Pilgrim Hiuen Tsang.

    S_6 : He stayed there for several years.

    The correct sequence should be

    (a) QPSR   (b) RPSQ

    (c) SPQR   (d) RQPS   *[SSC CGL (Mains), 2015]*

5. S_1 : Shaw read the first few lines of the

    P : and was at once convinced

    Q : he sent a few copies of the book to well known

    R : that he was reading good poetry, so

    S : poem

    S_6 : critics and awaited their reaction.

    The correct sequence should be

    (a) PQSR   (b) SRQP

    (c) SPRQ   (d) QPRS   *[SSC CGL, 2012]*

6. S_1 : Plato's 'Republic' has exercised tremendous influence

    P : He states that statesmen should

    Q : on human thought and intelligence

    R : integrity because he felt that, only such men

S : be men of supreme intelligence and impeccable

S_6 : could enlighten the darker side of human nature into a
positive one.

The correct sequence should be

(a) RSQP   (b) QPSR

(c) RPSQ   (d) SQPR   *[SSC CGL, 2012]*

7. S_1 : These positive effects vary from genetic changes that

    P : to other related infections,

    Q : make us more resistant to the diseases responsible

    R : for epidemics and

    S : which have effects on humans that are

    S_6 : hard to pin down and quantify

The correct sequence should be

(a) RPQS   (b) QRPS

(c) SQPR   (d) PRSQ   *[SSC CGL, 2011]*

8. S_1 : After an entire generation of parents and teachers

    P : the level of depression

    Q : children's self-esteem, an indicator of good mental health

    R : has worked hard to improve its

    S : in young people has skyrocketed.

    S_6 : It is how we feel about ourselves,

The correct sequence should be

(a) PQRS   (b) QSRP

(c) RQSP   (d) SPRQ   *[SSC CGL, 2011]*

9. S_1 : Researchers say that jogging alone is unhealthy.

    P : It was found that communal joggers have double the number
of brain cells as solo runners.

    Q : These positive effects are suppressed when running occurs in
isolation.

    R : Experiments indicated that running alone stifles brain cell
regeneration.

    S : Experienced in a group, running stimulates brain cell growth.

    S_6 : However, joggers around the world should remember that
jogging is healthier than the rat race.

The correct sequence should be

(a) SPQR   (b) RPSQ

(c) RQPS   (d) PQSR   *[SSC CGL (Mains), 2015]*

10. S_1 : The heart is the pump of life.

    P : They have even succeeded in heart transplants.

    Q : Now-a-days surgeons are able to stop a patient's heart and carry out complicated operations.

    R : A few years ago, it was impossible to operate on a patient whose heart was not working properly.

    S : If the heart stops we die in about five minutes.

    S_6 : All this was made possible by the invention of the heart lung machine.

The correct sequence should be

(a) PQRS   (b) QRSP

(c) SRPQ   (d) SRQP   **[SSC CGL (Mains), 2015]**

Exercise 8

1. S_1 : Mandela led the battle of freedom against slavery.

    P : The way was fighting with non-violence and truth.

    Q : He fought it in a unique way.

    R : This struggle brought the racists down to the ground.

    S : Many nations got their freedom in this way.

    S_6 : But some nations still wouldn't get the desired freedom.

The correct sequence should be

(a) SPQR   (b) RSPQ

(c) PQRS   (d) QPRS   **[SSC CGL (Mains), 2015]**

2. S_1 : Jai alai is a hand-ball type game.

    P : In fact, this game originated in the Basque region of Spain.

    Q : And in Florida it is legal to place bets on the players of Jai alai.

    R : It is one of the fastest-moving ball games.

    S : Although, played quite well in Florida and Latin America, it is not an American game.

    S_6 : Sports experts agree that Jai alai requires more skill, speed, endurance and nerve than any other game.

The correct sequence should be

(a) PSRQ   (b) PSQR

(c) SRPQ   (d) SPQR   **[SSC CPO, 2011]**

3. S_1 : Grandpa had some old clothes.

    P : But my mother took them out and kept them neatly folded in the cupboard again.

Q : So, he threw them into the waste basket.

R : So, he put the clothing into the family's bag of items to donate to charity.

S : My mother found them and put them back in his basket.

S_6 : Grandpa finally put the items in my mother's mending basket and never saw them again.

The correct sequence should be

(a) SRPQ   (b) QSRP

(c) PQSR   (d) RSQP   *[SSC CGL (Mains), 2015]*

4. S_1 : The world is stunned with the news that 44 years old Steve Irwin is no more.

P : He was shooting in the Great Barrier Reef of Queensland.

Q : He was killed by the poisoned barb of a huge sting ray.

R : The incident took place at about 11 am.

S : He was shooting an underwater documentary.

S_6 : Irwin was brought to the surface unconscious.

The correct sequence should be

(a) QSPR   (b) PRSQ

(c) RSPQ   (d) SPQR   *[SSC CGL (Mains), 2015]*

5. S_1 : A couple in my neighbourhood is known for shouting at each other.

P : With an apprehension of a serious fight between the two I went closer to the door and peeped in.

Q : I intended to calm them down.

R : I could guess both of them lay peacefully in their bed.

S : Last night at about 11 o'clock I could hear shrieks and sounds.

S_6 : The fight was going on in a TV serial on a channel.

The correct sequence should be   *[SSC CGL (Mains), 2015]*

(a) PSRQ   (b) RPSQ

(c) SPQR   (d) RPQS

6. S_1 : Katherine Mansfield was born in Wellington, New Zealand.

P : In 1908, she went back to the London which she felt to be her spiritual home.

Q : She was sent to Queen's a College School London in her fifteenth year to finish her education.

R : She remained there for four years

S : Soon after returning to New Zealand, she became dissatisfied.

S_6 : She hoped to make a literary career there.

The correct sequence should be

(a) PSRQ   (b) PQRS

(c) QRSP   (d) RSQP   *[SSC CGL (Mains), 2015]*

7. S_1 : Designing is as natural to me as breathing.

P : It was then that I launched my own label.

Q : It's been a good season so far.

R : But my career took off only after the birth of my second child.

S : Right now, I'm busy with my first store.

S_6: Next month, I'll be going to New York.

The correct sequence should be

(a) QRSP   (b) PSQR

(c) SQRP   (d) RPSQ   *[SSC CGL (Mains), 2015]*

8. S_1: Children like to celebrate their birthday.

P : In addition to birthday presents, they also receive greetings.

Q : It provides an opportunity for them to enjoy themselves with their friends.

R : The birthday presents also add to their joy.

S : Nobody can deny that company of friends is joyful.

S_6 : All these factors make birthday worth celebrating.

The correct sequence should be

(a) QRSP   (b) SRPQ

(c) QSRP   (d) RPQS   *[SSC CGL (Mains), 2015]*

9. S_1 : The world leaders.

P : That the despotic regime will try to get.

Q : By unleashing cruder violence that may come.

R : Gathered in the peace conference were unanimous in voicing their fears.

S : Over its palpable sense of insecurity.

S_6 : in the form of the use of chemical weapons.

The correct sequence should be

(a) PQSR   (b) SQRP

(c) QPRS   (d) RPSQ   *[SSC CGL (Mains), 2015]*

10. S_1 : For seventeen years, she led a sheltered life in the convent.

S_6 : Two years later, she left the Loreto Convent where she had spent many happy and useful years.

P : Her heart went out to the people living there.

Q : In 1946, she asked for permission to work in the slums.

R : Then one day, while she was returning from an errand, she saw the slums of Kolkata.

S : She felt she had found her second vocation, her real calling.

The correct sequence should be

(a) PRSQ
(b) RPSQ
(c) RPQS
(d) QRPS　　　　　　　　　*[CDS, 2016]*

Exercise 9

1. S_1 : The Pyramids are beautiful enormous structures.

P : A mummy is the dead body of a human being to which oils and spices have been applied to prevent if from decaying.

Q : They are the tombs of the old kings of Egypt who were called the Pharaohs.

R : These mummies were placed inside these great Pyramids.

S : The bodies of the Pharaohs were made into mummies when they died.

S_6 : Near them were placed, gold, silver, food, furniture and other things because it was believed that the mummies might require them after death.

The correct sequence should be

(a) QPRS
(b) QSRP
(c) SPRQ
(d) QSPR　　　*[SSC CGL (Mains), 2015]*

2. S_1 : Once upon a time I went to Scotland.

P : I found my flesh creep as I walked down its sinister corridor.

Q : There, in a castle in the dark, misty highlands, actually a modest hotel in Edinburgh.

R : And the next, morning he'd been found with his throat slit.

S : We'd had dinner with Jock MC Arthur only the previous night,

S_6 : The chill finger of suspicion pointed at all of us.

The correct sequence should be

(a) QRSP
(b) PQSR
(c) QPSR
(d) SRQP　　　*[SSC CGL (Mains), 2015]*

3. S_1 : The most vulnerable section of the society are the students.

P : Revolutionary and new fledged ideas have a great appeal to them.

Q : Agitations may be non-violent methods of protest.

R : They cannot resist the charm of persuasion.

S : They are to be taught that without discipline they cannot get proper education.

S₆ : However if these become violent, the antisocial elements get encouraged and they put all proper working out of gear.

The correct sequence should be

(a) PRSQ   (b) RSQP

(c) SRPQ   (d) RPQS   *[SSC CGL, 2010]*

4. S_1 : Venice is a strange city.

P : There are about 400 odd bridges connecting the islands of Venice.

Q : There are no motor cars, no horses and no buses there.

R : These small islands are close to one another.

S : It is not one island, but a hundred islands.

S_6 : This is because Venice has no streets.

The correct sequence should be

(a) SRPQ   (b) PSRQ

(c) RQPS   (d) QSRP   *[SSC CGL, 2010]*

5. S_1 : American idealism is essentially a belief in the idea of progress.

S_6 : This sense they have inherited from the English.

P : Therefore, he believes that, because of human effort, the future will be better than the past.

Q : But if Americans are usually optimistic, they are not wholly unrealistic.

R : The American tends to view history as a record of human achievement.

S : They have some common sense practicality.

The correct sequence should be

(a) PQRS   (b) PQSR

(c) RPQS   (d) PRQS   *[NDA & NA, 2015]*

6. S_1 : The lions used to be widely distributed in Africa and Asia

S_6 : no hunting is permitted in such reserved areas.

P : there are special forest zones set aside for wildlife in various countries

Q : indiscriminate killing by hunters has been the cause of this drastic fall in their numbers

R : today they are a relatively rare species

S : if the species survives at all, it will be only in National Parks

The correct sequence should be

(a) RSQP   (b) SQRP
(c) RQSP   (d) SRPQ   *[CDS, 2014]*

7. S_1 : One of the gifts of independence is the awakening of women of our country.

    P : Besides, their talent is recognised and they are appointed to high posts in the state.

    Q : Free India has seen women as Governors, Ministers and Ambassadors.

    R : That is because our government is making efforts to raise their status.

    S : Women have a bright future in independent India.

    S_6 : We even had a women Prime Minister.

The correct sequence should be

(a) SPQR   (b) SRPQ
(c) QSPR   (d) QPSR   *[SSC CGL (Mains), 2015]*

8. S_1 : Technology is meant for bringing comfort to the body and spirituality brings comfort to the mind.

    P : But in India that never happened, religion has always encouraged Science.

    Q : Scientists were persecuted.

    R : Here religion and philosophy were never isolated practices.

    S : In the West, religion was always opposed to Science,

    S_6 : They intertwined with life, in music, art drama, dance, painting and sculpture.

The correct sequence should be

(a) PQSR   (b) PRSQ
(c) SQPR   (d) SRQP   *[SSC CGL (Mains), 2015]*

9. S_1 : The machines that drive modern civilisation derive their power from coal and oil.

    S_6 : Nuclear energy may also be effectively used in this respect.

    P : But they are not inexhaustible.

    Q : These sources may not be exhausted very soon.

    R : A time may come when some other sources have to be tapped and utilised.

    S : Power may, of course, be obtained in future from forests, water, wind and withered vegetables.

The correct sequence should be

(a) PQRS   (b) QPRS
(c) SRQP   (d) SPQR   *[NDA & NA, 2015]*

10. S_1 : Albert Edward did very well.

   S_6 : he then appointed a manager to take care of it.

   P : he started looking for a place to open the new shop

   Q : he started his shop with great enthusiasm

   R : he did so well that he began to think of opening another shop

   S : one fine morning, he found it on a nearby street

   The correct sequence should be

   (a) PQRS   (b) RSPQ

   (c) RPSQ   (d) PSRQ   *[CDS, 2012]*

Exercise 10

1. S_1 : Proud Little Astronomer sees a huge dragon in the Moon.

   P : Big Astronomer calls him and shows him the fly.

   Q : He runs to the Big Astronomer and calls him home,

   R : He is very excited and remembers his rival Big Astronomer.

   S : Big Astronomer agrees and later discovers a fly in the telescope lens.

   S_6 : Little Astronomer is shamefaced and becomes humble.

   The correct sequence should be

   (a) RQSP   (b) PQRS

   (c) RSPQ   (d) QPSR   *[SSC CPO, 2011]*

2. S_1 : Some say that failure is like toxic waste.

   P : I see failure more as a fertilizer.

   Q : Thinking about it pollutes and undermines the attitudes needed for success.

   R : The seeds of success must be planted afresh.

   S : It can be used to enrich the soil of your mind.

   S_6 : Turning failure into a fertilizer is accomplished by using your erros as steps in learning.

   The correct sequence should be

   (a) SRQP   (b) PQSR

   (c) SPQR   (d) QPSR   *[SSC CGL, 2010]*

3. S_1 : This was an important day for Al at took.

   P : It was a cold day, but Al at took would be warm.

   Q : For the first time he was going to hunt seals alone.

   R : First he put on his fur-lined jacket.

S : Then he put on mittens and boots of deer skin to protect his hands and feet from the cold.

S_6 : Finally, he picked up the gun he had cleaned so carefully the day before.

The correct sequence should be

(a) PQRS   (b) QPRS

(c) PRSQ   (d) QRPS   *[SSC CGL, 2010]*

4. S_1 : India is rapidly coming under the influence of Western culture.

P : Earlier India had its own moral and social values.

Q : This change can be seen in our education system, marriages, food habits and daily routine.

R : But today, they have changed enormously.

S : The effect of Westernisation is visible everywhere in India.

S_6 : It may be harmful to forget our culture and values completely.

The correct sequence should be

(a) SPRQ   (b) PQSR

(c) PSRQ   (d) QSRP   *[SSC CGL (Mains), 2015]*

5. S_1 : The detective walked into the dark room alone

S_6 : he carefully picked up the gun making sure not to smudge the fingerprints.

P : it was later that he found the gun lying under a chair

Q : first he felt for the switch and turned on the light

R : the furniture was smashed and the curtains torn

S : at once he saw the disorder and confusion in the room

The correct sequence should be

(a) SQPR   (b) PQRS

(c) QSRP   (d) RPSQ   *[CDS, 2013]*

6. S_1 : Love is one of the earliest of human passions.

P : It is also one of the sweetest

Q : Love should be directed towards a worthy object.

R : But, like all strong passions it may, if not well regulated and controlled, lead us into misery.

S : Or it will prove in the end a source of bitterness.

S_6 : Love, moreover, looks forward to reciprocation.

The correct sequence should be

(a) RQPS   (b) PRQS

(c) PQSR   (d) QRPS   *[SSC CPO, 2010]*

7. S_1: One of my friends Krishnan went to live in a village.

    P : But it was a very slow animal.

    Q : So Krishnan bought a donkey for 200 rupees.

    R : One day, his new neighbour told him that he must buy a donkey.

    S : Every family there had a donkey to carry things for them.

    S_6: It did not like to work.

The correct sequence should be

(a) SQPR   (b) RSQP

(c) QPRS   (d) PRSQ   *[SSC CPO, 2010]*

8. S_1 : The next morning, I found myself somewhat refreshed, but very hungry.

    P : I asked him to let me help unload the vessel.

    Q : I noticed I was near a large ship.

    R : I went at once to the captain.

    S : It was unloading a cargo of pig iron.

    S_6 : I wanted to earn money for food.

The correct sequence should be

(a) PQRS   (b) QSRP

(c) PRSQ   (d) SRPQ   *[SSC CPO, 2010]*

9. S_1 : Today, the Earth has many satellites besides the moon.

    P : But the pull of the Earth keeps them from doing so.

    Q : The artificial satellites do not fall because they are going too fast to do so.

    R : They are the artificial satellites made by man and very much smaller than the moon.

    S : As they speed along they tend to go straight off into space.

    S_6: As a result, they travel in an orbit round the Earth.

The correct sequence should be

(a) QPSR   (b) PRQS

(c) SPQR   (d) RQSP   *[SSC CPO, 2010]*

10. S_1 : In 1739, Nadir Shah, the mighty king of Iran, invaded India.

    S_6 : another trophy he took with him was the Peacock Throne built by Shahjahan.

    P : after a stay of two months, Nadir Shah went back to Iran

    Q : he defeated the Mughal army in the battle at Karnal

R : he took with him immense wealth as well as the Koh-i-Noor diamond

S : This was followed by the cruel massacre and reckless plunder of Delhi

The correct sequence should be

(a) QSPR   (b) RQPS

(c) PRQS   (d) SPRQ   *[CDS, 2013]*

Exercise 11

1. S_1 : Computers have infiltrated into all aspects of life.

P : This shows that the computer has become all-powerful.

Q : So it is with many other things where computers are indispensable.

R : City traffic, airline booking and air-traffic are all computer-controlled.

S : In such a situation, computer breakdown means the breakdown of the system it controls.

S_6 : Such is our dependence on it.

The correct sequence should be

(a) RQSP   (b) SQPR

(c) PQRS   (d) RPQS   *[SSC CPO, 2011]*

2. S_1 : Carpentry is a very strenuous profession.

P : Because of such tools they put themselves at risk of injury.

Q : In such areas, it is all too easy to fall or slip.

R : Sometimes their work demands climbing on high rise buildings.

S : Carpenters have to work with sharp tools.

S_6 : Their lives, thus, are full of challenges.

The correct sequence should be

(a) SPRQ   (b) PQSR

(c) RPSQ   (d) SQPR   *[SSC CPO, 2011]*

3. S_1 : In ancient times, a King named Sagar performed the 'Ashwamedha yagna'.

P : No one could capture the horse.

Q : Many tried to capture the horse.

R : As per rules a splendid horse was let loose and allowed to wander.

S : Those who tried had to fight, Sagar's warriors.

S_6 : Thus, Sagar's fame spread far and wide.

The correct sequence should be

(a) RSPQ   (b) RQPS

(c) RQSP   (d) QPRS   [SSC CPO, 2011]

4. S_1: Albert Edward had never liked the new vicar.

P : He wasn't the type of man they wanted with a classy congregation.

Q : And now he straightened himself a little.

R : He knew his value.

S : He'd said from the beginning that they had made a mistake.

S_6: He wasn't going to allow himself to be put upon.

The correct sequence should be

(a) PSQR   (b) QRPS

(c) SPQR   (d) SRPQ   [SSC CPO, 2011]

5. S_1 : Mr Sherlock Holmes and Dr Watson were spending a weekend in a University town.

S_6 : It was clear that something very unusual happened.

P : One evening, they received a visit from an acquaintance, Mr Hilton Soames.

Q : On that occasion, he was in a state of great agitation.

R : They were staying in furnished rooms, close to the library.

S : Mr Soames was a tall, thin man of a nervous and excitable nature.

The correct sequence should be

(a) PRSQ   (b) RPSQ

(c) PQRS   (d) RPQS   [NDA & NA, 2015]

6. S_1 : Rola Sleiman parked her car in the only empty spot outside Tripoli's Evangelical church.

P : But that's not the only thing that makes her unique.

Q : She's a pastor and at 37, she's younger than most of her colleagues.

R : It is a small sand-coloured building with a simple facade and large wooden doors in the middle of the city.

S : It was Sunday morning and like every Sunday at around this time, Rola was headed to work.

S_6 : Rola is also, as far as she knows, the only female pastor in Lebanon–and perhaps even in the entire Middle East.

The correct sequence should be

(a) PRSQ   (b) SQPR

(c) SRPQ   (d) RSQP   *[SSC CGL (Mains), 2015]*

7. S_1 : Of men's earliest inventions we know very little

S_6 : once man had fire, he was the master of all lower creatures.

P : man used stick and stone long before he dared to meddle with fire

Q : the first was to use a stone to crack a nut

R : the next was the use of a stick to strike an enemy

S : It was only a step further that he made a rude weapon by fastening a stone to the end of a stick

The correct sequence should be

(a) PQRS   (b) QRSP

(c) SPRQ   (d) SRQP   *[CDS, 2013]*

8. S_1 : Last night, I was very tired and dropped off to sleep

S_6 : a goat was chewing up my rose plants.

P : I thought I heard somebody move outside

Q : all of a sudden, a slight noise disturbed my sleep

R : I got out of bed quietly and peeped out of the window

S : I was frightened

The correct sequence should be

(a) QPRS   (b) QSPR

(c) SPQR   (d) RSPQ   *[CDS, 2013]*

9. S_1 : It was a very pleasant walk along the banks of the river

S_6 : it charmed me beyond measure.

P : the buffalo had huge horns

Q : a kind of unknown calm and peace seemed to slide into my soul

R : what delighted me most was the sight of a little boy sitting on the last buffalo in the herd

S : I saw a herd of buffaloes swimming across the river

The correct sequence should be

(a) SRPQ   (b) QSRP

(c) PQRS   (d) RPQS   *[CDS, 2013]*

10. S_1 : A reporter is someone who gathers and writes news

S_6 : the reporter and the editor are both called newsmen.

P : an editor is someone who prepares all the news for printing in the newspaper

Q : a reporter cannot do a good job unless he has a good understanding of the requirements of the editor of his newspaper

R : the editor decides how important each news story is and where it should be placed

S : many editors are former reporters

The correct sequence should be

(a) QPRS   (b) QRSP

(c) PRQS   (d) RSPQ   *[CDS, 2013]*

Exercise 12

1. S_1 : Our pleasures should be healthy so that they can impart a sense of well-being.

P : This applies very much to the passion for sports.

Q : Some people become slaves to an enthusiasm and regard it as their real and only pleasure in life.

R : It is quite possible that indulging this passion is doing them great harm.

S : Modern sports have become so exaggerated that they can damage and sometimes destroy one's health.

S_6 : An enthusiasm for violet sports may well dig an early grave for the participant.

The correct sequence should be

(a) QSPR   (b) QPRS

(c) QRSP   (d) QRPS   *[SSC CGL (Mains), 2015]*

2. S_1 : Great quantities of animal oil come from whales

S_6 : a few other creatures also yield oil.

P : it produces a great quantity of oil which can be made into food for human consumption

Q : these enormous creatures of the sea are the largest remaining animals in the world

R : when the whale is killed, the blubber is stripped off and boiled down

S : to protect the whales from the cold of the Arctic seas, nature has provided it with a thick covering of fat called blubber

The correct sequence should be

(a) PSRQ   (b) QSRP

(c) PRQS   (d) RPQS   *[CDS, 2014]*

3. S_1 : We who live in the present day world are proud to call ourselves civilised

S_6 : in fact science has added to our worries.

P : but let us search our hearts and ask ourselves, 'Has science solved our problem?'

Q : is it because we live and dress better than our forefathers?

R : frankly speaking, the answer is 'No'

S : of course, we have the advantages of the inventions of science which our ancestors had never known

The correct sequence should be

(a) PQRS   (b) QSPR

(c) PRSQ   (d) SPRQ   *[CDS, 2014]*

4. S_1 : No daily paper has ever found its way into this village.

S_6 : they carry this with them to the trading centres in the plains and cities.

P : these travellers come from distant places,

Q : on their return journey they have news from the hills

R : The only news the inhabitants get is from travellers,

S : on their way into the hills they bring news from distant plains and cities of India,

The correct sequence should be

(a) PQSR   (b) RPSQ

(c) QSPR   (d) RQPS   *[CDS, 2013]*

5. S_1 : Why do birds migrate in spite of the heavy loss of life on the way?

S_6 : the migration of birds thus is a fascinating study, indeed.

P : but, birds also migrate during summer

Q : primarily, they migrate during the winter

R : also, they cannot endure the summer heat

S : and the main reason now is not hunger but availability of the nesting sites

The correct sequence should be

(a) QPSR   (b) PQRS

(c) RSPQ   (d) QRPS   *[CDS, 2012]*

6. S_1 : When Madhu opened the living room, an extraordinary sight met her eyes

 S_6 : hurrying upstairs, she went to her dressing table but to her relief found that the man had taken only an imitation diamond necklace.

 P : She soon returned home in a police car with two policemen

 Q : a strange man was fast asleep in an armchair.

 R : Madhu left the house immediately and went to the police station,

 S : but it was now too late, the man had disappeared

The correct sequence should be

(a) RPQS   (b) QRPS

(c) PQRS   (d) SQRP   *[CDS, 2013]*

7. S_1 : When Galileo was young, people believed that the Earth was the centre of the Universe

 S_6 : but time has proved that Galileo's view was right.

 P : but Galileo began to argue that it was not so

 Q : this belief was supported by the state and the Church

 R : he said that the Earth and other planets moved round the Sun

 S : he was imprisoned for voicing this unorthodox view

The correct sequence should be

(a) PQRS   (b) QPRS

(c) QPSR   (d) PSRQ   *[CDS, 2013]*

8. S_1 : One winter afternoon she had been buying something in a little antique shop in Curzon street

 S_6 : he clasped his hands, he was so gratified he could scarcely speak.

 P : therefore she visited this shop once again

 Q : It was a shop she always liked to visit-

 R : he beamed whenever she came in

 S : and the man who kept it was very fond of serving her

The correct sequence should be

(a) PSQR   (b) QPSR

(c) PRQS   (d) QSPR   *[CDS, 2013]*

9. S_1 : In our youth, we are apt to think that applause and publicity constitute success.

    S_6 : So let us be initiated into the mysteries of maturity and be taught how to resist and spurn the lure of hollow shows.

    P : The man who values the applause more than his own effort has not outgrown his youth.

    Q : It is our achievement or work which wins lasting rewards.

    R : But these are only the trappings, the ephemeral illusions.

    S : One should concentrate on one's work knowing that applause will come unsought.

The correct sequence should be

(a) SRQP   (b) PSRQ

(c) QPSR   (d) RQPS   *[CDS, 2016]*

10. S_1 : Wordsworth knew the behaviour of owls in the night better than most of us know the ways of black birds in day time.

    S_6 : His great poetry owes much to the night.

    P : Out of school there were no restrictions on the hours he kept.

    Q : No poet ever had happier school days.

    R : He would skate by the light of the stars, snare woodcocks at dead of night, watch the sunrise after a log ramble.

    S : Throughout life he was an inveterate walker by night.

The correct sequence should be

(a) QPRS   (b) PSQR

(c) QRPS   (d) SQPR   *[CDS, 2016]*

Exercise 13

1. S_1 : Forests have an influence on the climate of a region,

    S_6 : thus, we see that forests in a region often make climate cooler

    P : much of the rain that falls beneath the trees dissolves plant food in the soil,

    Q : this gives to the air over the forests a coolness which is felt by balloonists and aviators three thousand feet above the Earth

    R : the plants absorb all the food and much of the water, but the rest of the water is breathed out through the leaves into the air.

    S : this is taken up by the roots of plants and carried upward to the leaves

The correct sequence should be

(a) QSRP   (b) PSRQ

(c) RSPQ   (d) SQPR   *[CDS, 2012]*

2. S_1 : The parents of Bose wanted him to become an ICS Officer

   S_6 : his resignation showed that his country's freedom was more important to him than his personal ambitions.

   P : but his heart was not for government service

   Q : he studied zealously and got through the ICS examination in the fourth rank

   R : soon he resigned from the ICS to the bewilderment of all

   S : very much against his will, he was sent to England

   The correct sequence should be

   (a) QRPS   (b) RPSQ

   (c) SQPR   (d) PSQR   *[CDS, 2013]*

3. S_1 : The train was running fast and the next station was nearly an hour ahead

   S_6 : she bought four cups of ice-cream and all of them became busy with eating.

   P : the children were pestering their aunt with embarrassing questions.

   Q : the occupants of the first carriage among others were a tall girl, a little girl and a little boy

   R : luckily an ice-cream vendor came to the rescue of the aunt

   S : their aunt was occupying a corner seat

   The correct sequence should be

   (a) PQRS   (b) QSPR

   (c) RPQS   (d) SRQP   *[CDS, 2013]*

4. S_1 : Until the hospital could be built there was no surgery available for the patients.

   S_6 : after a short time an emergency hospital was created from a rough fowl-house.

   P : but there were disadvantages.

   Q : Schweitzer therefore started his medical treatment in an open space outside his house

   R : moreover, there was a storm almost every evening, when everything had to be dragged hurriedly to the shelter of the verandah.

   S : Working in the Sun was very tiring

   The correct sequence should be

   (a) QRPS   (b) QPSR

   (c) RPSQ   (d) PRSQ   *[CDS, 2013]*

5. S_1 : Once upon a time, there was a king who had a wonderfully nice garden.

   S_6 : In the trees lived a nightingale that sang so sweetly that all who passed by stood still and listened.

   P : In the middle of the garden, there was a lovely forest with tall trees and deep lakes.

   Q : In this garden were to be seen the most wonderful flowers with silver bells tied to them.

   R : The garden was so large that even the gardener himself did not know where it began and where it ended.

   S : These bells always sounded so that nobody should pass by without noticing the flowers.

   The correct sequence should be

   (a) QPRS   (b) SPQR

   (c) QSRP   (d) QPSR   *[CDS, 2016]*

6. S_1 : What Martin Luther King, the peaceful warrior and his followers suffered, it is very difficult to describe

   S_6 : for they had taken an oath to 'refrain from the violence of the fist, tongue or heart'.

   P : the police used fire horses and ferocious dogs to rout them

   Q : the law courts sent them to solitary confinement where not a ray of the Sun entered

   R : they were abused and stoned by the mob, slapped and kicked by the police

   S : they suffered and tolerated all this without ever lifting a hand in self defence

   The correct sequence should be

   (a) SRPQ   (b) RPQS

   (c) PRSQ   (d) QRSP   *[CDS, 2014]*

7. S_1 : There are, I think, several factors that contribute to wisdom

   S_6 : you have not time to consider the effect which your discoveries or inventions may have outside the field of medicine.

   P : this has become more difficult than it used to be owing to the extent and complexity of the specialised knowledge required of various kinds of technicians

   Q : of these I should put first a sense of proportion : the capacity to take account of all the important factors in a problem and to attach to each its due weight

R : the work is difficult and is likely to absorb the whole of your intellectual energy

S : suppose, e.g. that you are engaged in research in scientific medicine

The correct sequence should be

(a) QPSR   (b) QRPS

(c) QSPR   (d) QSRP   *[CDS, 2014]*

8. S_1 : There were no finger prints anywhere

S_6 : these conclusions made the detectives think that it was a fake theft.

P : first of all, it was impossible even for a child to enter through the hole in the roof

Q : when the investigators tried to reconstruct the crime, they came up against facts

R : moreover, when the detectives tried to push a silver vase, it was found to be double the size of the hole

S : again, the size of the hole was examined by the experts who said that nothing had been passed through it

The correct sequence should be

(a) PQRS   (b) QPRS

(c) SQRP   (d) QRSP   *[CDS, 2014]*

9. S_1 : The authorities decided to streamline the procedure for admitting students, to the new course

S_6 : the selection was made from the list in the order of priority.

P : those who performed badly at the interview were eliminated

Q : the candidates were first required to take a written test

R : a list of successful candidates at the written test was prepared in the ascending order of total marks

S : the top fifty among those who qualified were called for an interview

The correct sequence should be

(a) QRSP   (b) PRSQ

(c) SRQP   (d) RSQP   *[CDS, 2012]*

10. S_1 : Good memory is so common that we regard a man who does not possess it as eccentric.

S_6 : She wheeled away the perambulator, picturing to herself his terror when he would come out and find the baby gone.

P : I have heard of a father who having offered to take the baby out in a perambulator, was tempted by the sunny morning to pause on his journey and slip into a public house for a glass of beer.

Q : A little later, his wife had to do some shopping which took her past the public house where to her horror, she discovered her sleeping baby.

R : Leaving the perambulator outside, he disappeared into the drink shop.

S : Indignant at her husband's behaviour, she decided to teach him a lesson.

The correct sequence should be

(a) PQRS   (b) PRQS

(c) PSQR   (d) PQSR   *[CDS, 2016]*

Exercise 14

1. S_1 : Her sisters recognised her at once

   S_6 : as for the young prince, he found her more lovely and lovable than ever and insisted upon marrying her immediately.

   P : she embraced them, telling them she forgave them with all her heart

   Q : then she departed with the herald to the King's palace

   R : they were not in the least surprised, for everybody believed in fairies and everybody longed to have a fairy Godmother

   S : she told her whole story to his Majesty and the royal family

   The correct sequence should be

   (a) RSQP   (b) QPSR

   (c) PQSR   (d) PSQR   *[CDS, 2013]*

2. S_1 : The wise men laughed at Galileo for presuming to differ from the great Aristotle

   S_6 : both struck the ground together, as he had asserted that they would.

   P : he then climbed to the top, carrying with him a ten pound shot and a one pound shot

   Q : So, one morning he took some students and teachers to the base of the famous Leaning Tower

   R : balancing them on the edge of the tower, he let them fall together

   S : But Galileo said he could prove his statement

The correct sequence should be

(a) SQPR   (b) QPSR

(c) PRSQ   (d) RSQP   **[CDS, 2013]**

3. S_1 : The Earth was initially very hot and without an atmosphere

  S_6 : but it contained a lot of other gases that are poisonous to us.

  P : the atmosphere came from the emission of gases from the rocks

  Q : because it contained no oxygen

  R : in the course of time it cooled and acquired an atmosphere

  S : this early atmosphere was not one in which we could have survived

The correct sequence should be

(a) RPSQ   (b) PSRQ

(c) SPQR   (d) QRPS   **[CDS, 2013]**

4. S_1 : You ask me what I intend to do after graduation

  S_6 : that would be a great relief to my parents.

  P : my ambition is to become an engineer

  Q : I can complete this course in two years

  R : but, I am not sure whether I shall get enough marks to qualify for admission to an engineering college

  S : If I don't take up engineering, I would like to do an MSc in Physics

The correct sequence should be

(a) PRSQ   (b) SQPR

(c) QSRP   (d) RPQS   **[CDS, 2012]**

5. S_1 : In 1974, Mark and Delia ventured into the Kalahari desert to study the ecology of the region

  S_6 : she was moving towards them from about five metres away, her head swaying from side to side

  P : he slowly lifted his head and surveyed the scene

  Q : a soft groan startled Mark

  R : they had driven North the evening before, trying to locate the roars of a lion

  S : his breath caught—it was a huge lioness

The correct sequence should be

(a) RQPS   (b) RPQS

(c) RQSP   (d) QPSR   **[CDS, 2012]**

6. S_1 : At the roadside, the driver will be asked to blow through a small glass tube into a plastic bag.

S_6 : The driver will be asked to go to the police station.

P : And if the colour change does not reach the line the driver cannot be punished under the new law.

Q : Inside the tube are chemically treated crystals which change colour if the driver has alcohol on his breath.

R : But if the colour change does reach the line then the test has proved positive.

S : If the colour change goes beyond a certain line marked on the tube, this indicates that the driver is probably drunk over the specified limit.

The correct sequence should be

(a) PSQR   (b) SQRP

(c) RPSQ   (d) QSPR   *[NDA & NA, 2015]*

7. S_1 : One of the most terrible battles of the American Civil War was fought in July, 1863, at Gettysburg.

P : The chief speech on that occasion was given by Edward Everett, a celebrated orator.

Q : Lincoln was asked to make a few remarks.

R : In November of that year a portion of the battlefield was dedicated as a final resting place for men of both armies who died there.

S : Everett's speech lasted 2 hours. Lincoln's for 2 minutes; it was over almost before the crowd realised that it had begun.

S_6 : But the Gettysburg speech is now one of the world's immortal pieces of literature.

The correct sequence should be

(a) SQRP   (b) RPQS

(c) PQRS   (d) QPSR   *[SSC CGL, 2010]*

8. S_1 : My office sent an urgent e-mail asking me to return.

S_6 : It was evening before, I could sit and write to my parents that I would be joining them soon.

P : I immediately replied requesting a few days of grace as I had to book the return passage, pack and attend sundry matters before winding up my establishment here.

Q : On the way, I went to be laundry and made sure I would get my clothes in time.

R : Then I rushed to the bank, collected all my money and made reservations for my return journey.

S : From the shop next to it, I bought a couple of trunks to dump my books and other odd articles so that I could send them away in advance.

The correct sequence should be

(a) PQRS   (b) PRQS

(c) PRSQ   (d) PSRQ   *[CDS, 2016]*

9. S_1 : Science has already conferred an immense boon on mankind by the growth of medicine.

S_6 : The general death rate in 1948 (10·8) was the lowest ever recorded up to that date.

P : It has continued ever since and is still continuing.

Q : In the 18th century, people expected most of their children to die before they were grown-up.

R : In 1920, the infant mortality rate in England and Wales was 80 per thousand; in 1948 it was 34 per thousand.

S : Improvement began at the start of the 19th century, chiefly owing to vaccination.

The correct sequence should be

(a) RPQS   (b) QSPR

(c) SQRP   (d) PQSR   *[CDS, 2016]*

10. S_1 : The young traveller gazed out into the dismal country with a face of mingled repulsion and interest.

S_6 : He quickly restored it to his secret pocket.

P : At intervals, he drew from his pocket a bulky letter to which he referred and on the margins of which he scribbled some notes.

Q : It was a navy revolver of the largest size.

R : From the back of his waist he produced something which one would hardly have expected to find in the possession of so mild-mannered a man.

S : As he turned it slantwise to the light, the glint upon the rims of the copper shells within the drum showed that it was fully loaded.

The correct sequence should be

(a) PQRS   (b) RPQS

(c) QPRS   (d) PRQS   *[CDS, 2016]*

1. S_1 : Human ways of life have steadily changed.

S_6 : Even if we try to do nothing, we cannot prevent change.

P : Ancient Egypt-Greece-the Roman Empire-the Dark Ages and the Middle Ages-the Renaissance-the age of modern science and of modern nations one has succeeded the other, the history has never stood still.

Q : About ten thousand years ago, man lived entirely by hunting.

R : A settled civilised life only began when agriculture was discovered.

S : From that time to this, civilisation has always been changing.

The correct sequence should be

(a) QRSP   (b) QPSR

(c) QSRP   (d) PRSQ   *[CDS, 2016]*

2. S_1 : One of the first things the learning of a new language teaches you is that language comes from the region of the unconscious.

S_6 : The test of how much you know is : how much can you say without having to think how you are going to say it?

P : What is often meant by 'thinking in a language' is really the ability to use it without thinking about it.

Q : We, grown-up people, have to filter it through our minds-a much more laborious process.

R : That is why children learn a new language so effortlessly : it comes straight from their instincts.

S : But we cannot say that we know a language, or know what we have studied of it, until we can use it instinctively.

The correct sequence should be

(a) SQRP   (b) RPSQ

(c) PQSR   (d) RQSP   *[CDS, 2016]*

3. S_1 : But at that moment, I glanced round at the crowd that had followed me.

P : It was an immense crowd two thousand at the least and growing every minute

Q : They were watching me as they would watch a conjurer about to perform a trick

R : I looked at the sea of yellow faces above the garish clothes-faces all happy and excited over this bit of fun all certain that the elephant was going to be shot.

S : It blocked the road for a long distance on either side.

S_6 : They did not like me, but with the magical rifle in my hands, I was momentarily worth watching.

The correct sequence should be

(a) RPQS   (b) QSRP

(c) SRPQ   (d) PSRQ   *[SSC TA, 2009]*

4. S_1 : There are many roads into the world of books, but the way of fiction is probably the most common.

P : Then too the appeal of the story, whether told as poem play, history, biography or novel is primitive and strong.

Q : The reason is plain.

R : They are to us what epic poetry was to the Greeks and Romans, what the stage was to the Elizabethans.

S : The novel and the short story come closer to the experience of the modern reader than any other form of contemporary writing.

S_6 : Mankind's delight in stories is as timeless and universal as the art of the story teller.

The correct sequence should be

(a) QSRP   (b) SRPQ

(c) RSQP   (d) PRSQ   *[SSC TA, 2009]*

5. S_1 : 'Acu' means needles in Latin.

P : The needles stimulates specific nerves that transmit electrical impulses *via* the spinal cord and brain to the affected area.

Q : Quite appropriately, then, acupuncture consists of inserting very fine needles at specific points on the skin located near nerve endings.

R : Acupuncture also stimulates the release of chemical substances from the brain centres and pituitary glands.

S : These are connected to one another by lines called channels or meridians.

S_6 : Known as endorphins and encephalins, which are released and carried across the blood stream, these chemicals are the body's own pain-relief mechanism.

The correct sequence should be

(a) SPRQ   (b) RSQP

(c) PQRS   (d) QSPR   *[SSC CPO, 2006]*

6. S_1 : The dead do sometimes tell tales, if you know how to look for them.

    P : The flesh of bomb victims is shredded and may be sieged by chemicals.

    Q : In the autopsy rooms of the Suffolk county, the medical examiner and his team were looking for clues that could explain how the passengers of TWA Flight 800 died.

    R : But most of the corpses he examined had been killed by the impact of hitting the water from a height of more than two miles.

    S : The body of a person killed by a bomb looks different from the body of a victim in an ordinary plane crash.

    S_6 : The mystery of their deaths will be solved in time, but it won't be easy or quick.

The correct sequence should be

(a) SRQP   (b) PQRS

(c) QSPR   (d) RSPQ   **[SSC CPO, 2006]**

7. S_1 : In a first, a robotic exoskeleton device has enabled a 39 years old former athlete, who had been completely paralysed for 4 years.

    P : This is the first time that a person with chronic, complete paralysis has regained enough voluntary control to actively work with a robotic device.

    Q : The athlete's leg movement also resulted in other health benefits.

    R : To control his leg muscles and take thousand of steps.

    S : In addition to the device, the man was aided by a novel non-invasive spinal stimulation technique that does not require surgery.

    S_6 : Including improved cardiovascular function and muscle tone.

The correct sequence should be

(a) QRPS   (b) RPSQ

(c) SPQR   (d) PQRS   **[SSC CGL (Mains), 2015]**

8. S_1 : The distance between theatre and reality has stretched so far that when we come across a truly contemporary play, it is a cause for rejoicing.

    S_6 : but the question is, have we forgotten his legacy in modern India?

P : it searches our collective psyche like an unrelenting laser beam

Q : most importantly, the play questions whether religion and politics can fuse together in modern India

R : Gandhiji had both the spiritual and political dimensions that we so lack today

S : Prasanna's Gandhiji staged recently by the National School of Drama is one such play

The correct sequence should be

(a) SRPQ

(b) RSPQ

(c) SPQR

(d) RQPS

[CDS, 2014]

9. S_1 : Though hard to please and easily offended, Johnson had a most humane and benevolent heart.

S_6 : he got her a job and put her into a virtuous way of living.

P : there he discovered, she was one of those wretched persons who had fallen into the lowest state of vice, poverty and disease

Q : going home one evening, he found a poor woman lying in the street and took her upon his back and carried her to his house

R : soon, she was restored to health

S : Instead of harshly scolding her, he had taken care of her with all tenderness

The correct sequence should be

(a) PQRS

(b) SRQP

(c) PRQS

(d) QPSR

[CDS, 2012]

10. S_1 : There is no doubt that democracy is the best of the systems of government available to us.

S_6 : It is this feature that puts democracy in a class by itself among political systems.

P : for another, even an individual can, through appeal to the judiciary, prevent the government from doing any injustice

Q : this means that, in a way, the people can exercise some control over the rulers even during their period of rule

R : this right of the individual to secure justice even against powerful government is even more important than the right to vote

S : for one thing, it permits, if necessary, a periodical change of those who govern the country

The correct sequence should be

(a) RPQS

(b) SQPR

(c) PQRS

(d) SRPQ

[CDS, 2012]

Answers

Exercise 1

1. (d) **2.** (c) **3.** (b) **4.** (a) **5.** (c) **6.** (a) **7.** (c) **8.** (d) **9.** (c) **10.** (b)

Exercise 2

1. (c) **2.** (a) **3.** (d) **4.** (a) **5.** (b) **6.** (d) **7.** (a) **8.** (b) **9.** (c) **10.** (c)

Exercise 3

1. (a) **2.** (a) **3.** (c) **4.** (a) **5.** (d) **6.** (c) **7.** (d) **8.** (c) **9.** (c) **10.** (c)

Exercise 4

1. (b) **2.** (a) **3.** (b) **4.** (a) **5.** (a) **6.** (a) **7.** (a) **8.** (c) **9.** (d) **10.** (d)

Exercise 5

1. (a) **2.** (c) **3.** (b) **4.** (a) **5.** (c) **6.** (d) **7.** (b) **8.** (b) **9.** (d) **10.** (a)

Exercise 6

1. (a) **2.** (d) **3.** (a) **4.** (d) **5.** (b) **6.** (d) **7.** (d) **8.** (a) **9.** (c) **10.** (c)

Exercise 7

1. (b) **2.** (a) **3.** (c) **4.** (d) **5.** (c) **6.** (b) **7.** (b) **8.** (c) **9.** (b) **10.** (d)

Exercise 8

1. (d) **2.** (d) **3.** (d) **4.** (a) **5.** (c) **6.** (c) **7.** (d) **8.** (c) **9.** (d) **10.** (b)

Exercise 9

1. (d) **2.** (c) **3.** (a) **4.** (a) **5.** (c) **6.** (c) **7.** (b) **8.** (c) **9.** (b) **10.** (c)

Exercise 10

1. (a) **2.** (d) **3.** (b) **4.** (a) **5.** (c) **6.** (b) **7.** (b) **8.** (b) **9.** (d) **10.** (a)

Exercise 11

1. (a) **2.** (a) **3.** (c) **4.** (c) **5.** (b) **6.** (d) **7.** (b) **8.** (b) **9.** (b) **10.** (a)

Exercise 12

1. (d) **2.** (b) **3.** (b) **4.** (b) **5.** (a) **6.** (b) **7.** (b) **8.** (b) **9.** (d) **10.** (a)

Exercise 13

1. (b) **2.** (d) **3.** (b) **4.** (b) **5.** (c) **6.** (b) **7.** (d) **8.** (b) **9.** (a) **10.** (b)

Exercise 14

1. (c) **2.** (a) **3.** (a) **4.** (a) **5.** (a) **6.** (d) **7.** (b) **8.** (b) **9.** (b) **10.** (d)

Exercise 15

1. (a) **2.** (d) **3.** (d) **4.** (a) **5.** (d) **6.** (c) **7.** (b) **8.** (c) **9.** (d) **10.** (b)

Type III Para-Jumbles

Direction *Rearrange the following sentences in the correct sequence to form a meaningful paragraph, then answer the questions given below them.*

Exercise 1

1. A : for some time
   B : which is troublesome
   C : the weather becomes cool and pleasant
   D : though there is humidity in it
   The correct sequence should be
   (a) CBAD   (b) DBAC
   (c) ACBD   (d) CADB   *[SSC CGL (Mains), 2014]*

2. A : well skilled in his job
   B : he is a capable person
   C : but his roughness of a rustic nature
   D : devalues his achievements
   The correct sequence should be
   (a) BACD   (b) BCDA
   (c) CDBA   (d) ADBA   *[SSC CGL (Mains), 2014]*

3. A : he did not take revenge on Ravi
   B : though he had
   C : as he was magnanimous
   D : done great harm to him
   The correct sequence should be
   (a) BCAD   (b) CABD
   (c) BDAC   (d) ADCB   *[SSC CGL (Mains), 2014]*

4. A : have some influence on
   B : alter much of his natural bent
   C : no doubt, education and surroundings
   D : the direction of a man's life, but they do not
   The correct sequence should be
   (a) CBAD   (b) ADBC
   (c) DACB   (d) CADB   *[SSC CGL (Mains), 2014]*

5. A : his writings are so philosophical

    B : to read between the lines

    C : that it is sometimes difficult

    D : and find out what he wants to convey

The correct sequence should be

(a) ACBD   (b) BDAC

(c) BCAD   (d) ABCD   *[SSC CGL (Mains), 2014]*

6. A : just to prove

    B : disparaging each new production

    C : no one liked their caustically

    D : the playwright's worthlessness

The correct sequence should be

(a) DBAC   (b) CBAD

(c) CDAB   (d) ADBC   *[SSC CGL (Mains), 2014]*

7. A : although a great scientist

    B : Einstein was weak in arithmetic

    C : right from his school days

    D : it has been established that

The correct sequence should be

(a) DCBA   (b) ADBC

(c) DABC   (d) DBCA   *[SSC CGL (Mains), 2014]*

8. A : choice of goals that are not

    B : wisdom is equally needed

    C : only beneficient but also attainable

    D : in private life in the

The correct sequence should be

(a) ABCD   (b) BDAC

(c) CBDA   (d) ADCB   *[SSC CGL (Mains), 2014]*

9. A : has only spread to other parts of the world recently

    B : mango has been commercially cultivated

    C : for many years, although its cultivation

    D : in the Indo-Burma Malayan region of South-East Asia

The correct sequence should be

(a) ADBC   (b) BADC

(c) BDCA   (d) DACB   *[SSC CGL (Mains), 2014]*

10. A : people blame others for their misdeeds

    B : of the present-day world arise

    C : most of the troubles

    D : from the fact that instead of doing their duty

The correct sequence should be

(a) DCBA   (b) CBAD

(c) CBDA   (d) ABDC   *[SSC CGL (Mains), 2014]*

Exercise 2

1. A : inside the auditorium   B : other people

    C : apart from us   D : there were several

The correct sequence should be

(a) BDAC   (b) CBDA

(c) CDBA   (d) ABDC   *[SSC CGL (Mains), 2014]*

2. A : can make Indian farmers active

    B : growth of industries

    C : throughout the year

    D : in cities around the villages

The correct sequence should be

(a) DCAB   (b) BADC

(c) BDAC   (d) CADB   *[SSC CGL (Mains), 2014]*

3. A : a valuable aid to education

    B : the cinema offers

    C : not only amusement

    D : but also

The correct sequence should be

(a) BCDA   (b) BDAC

(c) CBDA   (d) DABC   *[SSC CGL (Mains), 2014]*

4. A : to raise to their status

    B : from others

    C : and to gain acceptance

    D : people follow fashion

The correct sequence should be

(a) DBCA   (b) ABCD

(c) DACB   (d) BCAD   *[SSC CGL (Mains), 2014]*

5. P : do or die was the call
   Q : that Gandhiji gave
   R : when he asked the British to quit India
   S : to all freedom fighters
The correct sequence should be

(a) QPRS   (b) PRQS
(c) RSPQ   (d) PQSR   **[CDS, 2011]**

6. P : on the propagation of the idea
   Q : of family planning
   R : the governments of many countries
   S : have been spending a lot of money
The correct sequence should be

(a) PQRS   (b) PSQR
(c) SPQR   (d) RSPQ   **[CDS, 2011]**

7. P : they did not grow well
   Q : although
   R : he watered the plants regularly
   S : and put manure in them
The correct sequence should be

(a) PQRS   (b) QRSP
(c) RSQP   (d) QPRS

8. A : They fled to the higher ground.
   B : Soon the floods retired and the villagers were able to return.
   C : The river overflowed its banks.
   D : The rain fell steadily for several days.
   E : The terrified villagers abandoned their homes.
The correct sequence should be

(a) CEBAD   (b) DEBCA
(c) DCEAB   (d) EDABC   **[MAT, 2013]**

9. A : like the industrialised countries
   B : as if they are to be suffered as relics of a backward past
   C : we have specially drawn attention to the non-motorised
       transport modes
   D : because they are completely overlooked in transport planning
   E : till replaced by faster petroleum fuelled transport
The correct sequence should be

(a) DEACB   (b) CDEBA
(c) CBADE   (d) CDBEA   **[MAT, 2011]**

10. A : he was highly sensitive and resentful
    B : towards the country or to those
    C : when there was even implied discourtesy
    D : while he was extremely gentle and tolerant
    E : he held in honour
    The correct sequence should be
    (a) ACDBE   (b) DACBE
    (c) EADCB   (d) DCBEA   *[MAT, 2011]*

Exercise 3

1. A : is different regions of that federation
   B : that was Yugoslavia
   C : the fundamental cause has been the very large difference in the quality of life
   D : although, the dismemberment of the federation
   E : is seen more as the result of an ethnic conflict
   The correct sequence should be
   (a) CEBDA   (b) DBECA
   (c) BCEDA   (d) ABDEC   *[MAT, 2011]*

2. A : but there is some merit in it
   B : as distinct from consumption
   C : the bifurcation of plan and non-plan funds
   D : in so far as it focuses attention on development expenses
   E : in the budget is artificial
   The correct sequence should be
   (a) DCABE   (b) CDBEA
   (c) CEABD   (d) DEACB   *[MAT, 2011]*

3. A : People started fearing a famine.
   B : Monsoon turned out to be unusually abundant and the danger was averted.
   C : The monsoon failed and water tanks became almost empty.
   D : So, no grain could be sown by the farmers in their fields.
   E : Farmers looked anxiously for the next monsoon.
   The correct sequence should be
   (a) CABDE   (b) CDAEB
   (c) AEDCB   (d) DABCE   *[MAT, 2013]*

4. A : Thus, despite India's huge population, we have not done well in Olympic Games.

   B : During the British period also, cricket remained popular in India.

   C : Cricket has been an extremely popular game in India for quite some time now.

   D : It is time our government and corporate fraternity pay due attention to other games/sports and we redeem our national pride in Olympic Games.

   E : However, due to this reason, other games/sports didn't receive the required attention they deserve.

The correct sequence should be

(a) EACDB   (b) BDACE

(c) CBEAD   (d) DCEAB   *[MAT, 2013]*

5. A : For pure vegetarians, India is a heaven.

   B : India can boast for its innumerable varieties of tasty and nutritious vegetarian dishes.

   C : These are also prepared using different methods of cooking like baking, boiling, frying etc.

   D : Vegetables are an integral part of our food and we consume them in a number of ways.

   E : Indians like their vegetable curries real hot 'n' spicy and so add a number of spices to make them really exotic.

The correct sequence should be

(a) BCADE   (b) AECDB

(c) CEBDA   (d) DABEC   *[MAT 2011]*

6. A : Economists all over the world have expressed anxiety in this regard.

   B : As a result, Indian people have been subjected to high cost of living and inflation.

   C : Indian economy has not shown desirable growth in the recent years.

   D : Grim global economic scenario has also contributed to this problem and it seems a quick fix solution is yet far away.

   E : But, one of the primary reasons for such a situation has been Indian Government's inability to take tough decision.

The correct sequence should be

(a) CAEBD   (b) ACDBE

(c) DEABC   (d) EADCB   *[MAT, 2013]*

7. A : Easy or not, etiquette is important.

    B : There's a reason for doing things the way we do them-we just have not idea what it is.

    C : I had to interrupt my cell phone call to tell him off.

    D : I was trying to explain this the other night to may children-Matt, 15 and Becky, 11-who, I'm ashamed to say, have been allowed to develop less than prefect manners, especially at the table.

    E : At this particular family dinner, I caught Matt buttering his baked potato with this finger.

The correct sequence should be

(a) ABCDE   (b) ABDEC

(c) BCDAE   (d) BDACE   *[MAT, 2012]*

8. A : "Are you all right"? I asked, as I helped her to her seat. "That turbulence was as bad as it gets."

    B : Flying the summer means one thing; turbulence.

    C : I was working as a flight attendant when we hit a patch of very rough air just after a young teenager, obviously on her first flight, had entered the bathroom.

    D : After the bumps had subsided, she exited the bathroom, a look of sheer terror etched on her face.

    E : "So that's what it was" she said, "I thought I'd pushed the wrong button."

The correct sequence should be

(a) DAEBC   (b) BCDAE

(c) AEBDC   (d) CADBE   *[MAT, 2012]*

9. A : But, transportation is difficult and the Pantanal is little known outside of Brazil.

    B : The people who live here have their fingers crossed.

    C : Because if ecotourism doesn't work, there is no alternative waiting.

    D : There are now some 60-odd tourist facilities here, most of them small and locally owned.

    E : Worldwide, the jury is still out on the idea of ecotourism and the Pantanal has become a testing ground.

The correct sequence should be

(a) EDABC   (b) DAEBC

(c) ECBAD   (d) EDCBA   *[MAT, 2012]*

10. A : And then suppose you pushed the 'Reverse' button and took a trip in the opposite direction-journeying into the dim recesses of the past.

B : Just suppose you could clamber aboard a Time Machine and press the 'Forward' button.

C : You might just land right into your favourite period of history.

D : Zap......would you hurtle forward through a blinding flash of days and nights, months and years-even long centuries-perhaps, to land into a alien world of the future...?

E : A world that will be a marvel of technology.

The correct sequence should be

(a) CDABE   (b) CBADE
(c) BDEAC   (d) BDECA   *[MAT, 2012]*

Exercise 4

1. A : Tasty and healthy food can help you bring out their best.

B : One minute they are toddlers and next you see them in their next adventure.

C : Your young ones seem to be growing so fast.

D : Being their loving custodians, you always want to see them doing well.

E : Their eyes sparkle with curiosity and endless questions on their tongues.

The correct sequence should be

(a) DBCEA   (b) CADEB
(c) CBEDA   (d) ECABD   *[MAT, 2015]*

2. A : Of course, the training was damn tough, both physically and mentally.

B : But, once he became fighter pilot in the Air Force, he was the happiest man going around.

C : As a child, watching flying aircraft was a passion for him.

D : So, he took the NDA exam to become a pilot in the Air Force.

E : He thought flying was the best career for him.

(a) DCBAE   (b) CEDAB
(c) BADEC   (d) EACDB   *[MAT, 2015]*

3. A : It is hoping that overseas friends will bring in big money and lift the morale of the people.

B : But a lot needs to be done to kick start industrial revival.

C : People had big hopes from the new government.

D : So far government has only given an incremental push to existing policies and programmes.

E : Government is to go for big time reforms, which it promised.

The correct sequence should be

(a) BCDAE (b) EADCB

(c) DABEC (d) CDEAB *[MAT, 2015]*

4. A : However, women hiring is catching up at a slow and steady rate in the recent times.

B : Gender ratio has been inclined more towards male employees.

C : As a result, recent reports have highlighted the rise in demand for women employees.

D : Women constitute a little over half of world's total population.

E : But, their contribution to measured economic activity is far below the potential.

The correct sequence should be

(a) DEBAC (b) CDAEB

(c) BCDEA (d) AEDBC *[MAT, 2015]*

5. A : A brain child to the Bihar Government, Bihar Diwas was first celebrated in 2010.

B : The State Government declared a holiday to mark the occasion.

C : On 22nd March, 2012, Bihar turned 100 years old, as on this day the British carved out the state in 1912.

D : Termed Bihar Diwas, the Government decorated the state capital with blue lights.

E : Now, Government has decided to celebrate this day every year with equal enthusiasm.

The correct sequence should be

(a) CEDAB (b) BDACE

(c) CBDAE (d) ECABD *[MAT, 2014]*

6. A : I studied at a premier convent school, where I was the athletics champion and the football captain.

B : School is a great leveller where you are known not by the money you have, but by how good you are in sport, not even studies.

C : My father is a Protestant and mother, an Iranian.

D : While I believe in the presence of a supreme being, I am agnostic.

E : From the age of four, my father always told me that 'to be a good man, you don't need to go to a temple, church or mosque, you just need to be good'.

The correct sequence should be

(a) DBACE   (b) CEDAB

(c) CEBDA   (d) BEACD   *[MAT, 2014]*

7. A : I refused to wear traditional wedding clothes, our backdrop was a caricature of the happy couple and there was no stage.

B : Even when I got married two years ago, my first idea for a reception was a pool party.

C : I am not a fan of Indian weddings.

D : That idea, of course, got rejected, but we did tinker with quite a few traditions and I did not wear a typical wedding dress.

E : Even now, friends tell us it was one of the best weddings they attended.

The correct sequence should be

(a) CEABD   (b) CBDAE

(c) BACDE   (d) BDACE   *[MAT, 2014]*

8. A : India, however, remains the front runner in economic growth in any cross-country comparison.

B : Political turmoil in the Middle East and rise in crude oil prices were other reasons for this situation.

C : For Indian economy, recovery was interrupted last year due to intensification of debt crisis in Euro zone.

D : As a result, growth moderated and fiscal balance deteriorated due to tight monetary policy and expanded outlays.

E : Monetary and fiscal policy response for better part of last three years aimed at taming domestic inflationary pressure.

The correct sequence should be

(a) CEDAB   (b) CBADE

(c) CEDBA   (d) CBAED   *[MAT, 2014]*

9. A : Environment education unit of centre for science.

B : Environment has always been working towards providing easy to understand reading material.

C : Their new publication on this subject is an attempt to lend teachers a helping hand.

D : It unfolds in two sections : *first*, Climate Change, how to make sense of it all and *second*, Natural Resources, how to share and care.

E : However, they are introduced to students not as a paragraph to memorise but as an activity to do.

The correct sequence should be

(a) ACEBD   (b) DBCAE
(c) ABCDE   (d) BECAD   *[MAT, 2013]*

10. A : A famous Japanese rock garden is at Ryoan ji in North-West Kyoto, Japan.

B : The rocks of various sizes are arranged on small white pebbles in five groups, each comprising, five, two, three, two and three rocks.

C : The garden in 30 m long from East to West and 10 m from North to South.

D : The garden contains 15 rocks arranged on the surface of white pebbles in such a manner that visitors can see only 14 of them at once from whichever angle the garden is viewed.

E : There are no trees, just around 15 irregularly shaped rocks of varying sizes, some around by rocks, arranged in a bed of white grancelsard that is ranked everyday.

The correct sequence should be

(a) ACEBD   (b) CAEDB
(c) DEABC   (d) BADEC   *[MAT, 2013]*

Exercise 5

1. A : From Sweden to the UK to Greece to even the US in the early part of the century, housing prices have fallen.

B : But wasn't that just correlation?

C : Housing bubbles have been known to go bust in the past and in different countries.

D : "The real estate market has never gone down in any meaningful way"— this statement was often quoted by real estate agents and brokers in the US and it might have even been statistically valid, with over 50 years of data supporting it.

E : While the argument is moot today (US House Prices are still falling, after more than three years of a downward trend) it remains alive in pockets of the world.

The correct sequence should be

(a) CDABE   (b) CDBAE
(c) DBCAE   (d) BEDAC   *[MAT, 2011]*

2. A : Environment Education Unit of Centre for Science and Environment has always been working towards providing easy-to-understand reading material.

   B : Their new publication on this subject is an attempt to lend teachers a helping hand.

   C : It unfolds in two sections : Climate Change: how to make sense of it all and Natural Resources : how to share and care.

   D : Here, the key issues selected adhere strictly to curriculum guidelines.

   E : However, they are introduced to students not as a paragraph to memorise, but as an activity to do.

The correct sequence should be

(a) ACEBD   (b) DBCAE

(c) ABCDE   (d) BECAD   *[MAT, 2012]*

6. A : For example, cars in the developing world are often seen as status symbols to be acquired, while in the developed world they are seen as liabilities to be discarded.

   B : The size of the carbon footprint of nations in the developing world has again come in for serious international discussion.

   C : The failed mission of Copenhagen is the immediate cause of the resumption of this debate.

   D : While the main triggers of the debate are economic, social and cultural factors also have a major role to play.

   E : As with so many other issues, clearly, here 'too one man's meat is another man's poison'.

(a) DECAB   (b) CEDAB

(c) BCDAE   (d) BACED   *[MAT, 2010]*

4. A : When they gathered together, the Buddha was completely silent and some speculated that perhaps the Buddha was tired or ill.

   B : It is said that Gautama Buddha gathered his disciples one day for a Dharma talk.

   C : One of the Buddha's disciples, Mahakasyapa, silently gazed at the flower and broke into a broad smile.

   D : The origins of Zen Buddhism are ascribed to the Flower Sermon, the earliest source for which come from the 14th century.

E : The Buddha silently held up and twirled a flower and twinkled his eyes; several of his disciples tried to interpret what this meant, though none of them was correct.

The correct sequence should be

(a) EBDAC   (b) DBAEC

(c) BCDEA   (d) CADBE   *[MAT, 2012]*

5. A : The band has gone through several drummers over the years, though Travis has held the position since 1989 and is the longest-serving.

B : 'Judas Priest' are an English heavy metal band from Birmingham, England, formed in 1969.

C : Their popularity and status as one of the definitive heavy metal bands has earned them the nickname 'Metal Gods' from their song of the same name.

D : They have been cited as an influence on many heavy metal musicians and bands.

E : The core line-up consists of lead vocalist Rob Halford guitarist Glenn Tipton, Bassist Ian Hill and Drummer Scott Travis.

The correct sequence should be

(a) ACBDE   (b) DABCE

(c) CDEAB   (d) BEADC   *[MAT, 2012]*

6. A : After all, a story told on the large screen inevitably differs from that told on the small screen.

B : This critical difference has an impact on viewership in term's of age, income and occupation.

C : In this age of the multimedia, we have to train ourselves to understand that as a rule, the medium is the message.

D : It also has an impact on the expectations brought by the public to bear on large and small screen performances and on the performers.

E : Never has the myth of 'one size fits all', been shown up so effectively, therefore, as in the field of Media Studies.

The correct sequence should be

(a) ABDCE   (b) CABED

(c) CABDE   (d) CDABE   *[MAT, 2012]*

7. A : Indeed, the reading-public of today seems to be more tolerant of this crossover than their predecessors might have been.

B : Both writers and readers seem to enjoy cross-crossing the line between documentation and fiction.

C : Beginning with Midnight's Children, there has been a steady breakdown of the disciplinary wall between literature and history.

D : Editorial cartoons, once barely recognised as a source of humour for the masses, are now studied as important sources of historical documentation and literary value.

E : This has led to a revision in the view of what constitutes historical and literary debate and of what constitutes the sources of this debate.

The correct sequence should be

(a) DECAB   (b) CBAED

(c) CABED   (d) ABCED   *[MAT, 2010]*

8. A : Sub-Saharan Africa is often cited as a territory in which starvation could be significantly reduced, were GM foods brought into worldwide circulation.

B : Farmers cite the steady impoverishment of the soil and the deterioration in the quality of seeds, as excellent reasons for protesting GM foods.

C : As with many cutting-edge discoveries, however, its long-term consequences can be difficult to handle.

D : Genetically modified or GM foods are marketed enthusiastically by some section of the developed world that claim they can cure the ills of the developing world.

E : A lack of transparency concerning ethical testing is another reason given by the developing world for receiving GM foods with caution rather than with celebration.

The correct sequence should be

(a) DACBE   (b) BEDCA

(c) CADEB   (d) DEBAC   *[MAT, 2010]*

9. A : Downshifting doesn't necessarily mean changing your job, but taking steps to stop your work taking over your life and it can involve flexible working.

B : This trend from the US, where it is practised by ten per cent of the working population, has arrived in India.

C : If you feel bored, frustrated and trapped in your job, you are a likely candidate for not just a job change but a downshift.

D : All of these things can lead to a better quality of life.

E : A better word for downshifting would be 're-equilibrating', suggests Judy Jones, co-author of 'Getting a life' 'the Down Shifter's Guide to a Happier, Simpler Living'.

The correct sequence should be

(a) EACBD   (b) AEDBC

(c) CBEAD   (d) AEBCD   *[MAT, 2016]*

10. A : To avoid either of these outcomes, they will weed to accumulate enough savings during their years in the workforce to support themselves with dignity for nearly twenty years after they are too old to work.

B : Most of India's 144 million informal sector workers who earn ₹ 3000 or less per month will become destitute as soon as they stop working.

C : But their fragile labour market attachments and modest intermittent incomes, coupled with the absence of a low cost secure long-term savings mechanism has effectively put retirement planning out of reach of India's working poor.

D : Income security in old age is rapidly emerging as one of the most important causes of poverty in India.

E : Or will be forced to work till they die.

The correct sequence should be

(a) ABDEC   (b) BADCE

(c) DBEAC   (d) DBAEC   *[MAT, 2016]*

Exercise 6

1. A : What was once marginal has now become central— the only possible strategy now is alliance, agreement, coalition and accommodation.

B : The shift to bottom-up political power has meant that India's reform 'agenda has become far more tentative, as policies can be derailed or slowed down by political parties with even small national clout.

C : Untrammeled acceptance of ineffective policies and bad ideas is no longer possible.

D : And, on the flip side coalition politics has worked its magic and India's potential bureaucrat-visionaries now have too many feet in the aisle ready to trip them over.

E : Since then, however India's democracy has changed and deepened.

The correct sequence should be

(a) ECDBA   (b) ACBED

(c) BEACD   (d) DECAB   *[MAT, 2016]*

2. A : The growth and activity of these NGOs is a sign of the changing nature of India's democracy.

   B : These organisations are emphasising an approach towards political democracy that is rooted in the idea of 'civil society' rather than in the divisions that now dominate India's politics.

   C : This ever-widening group of middle-class Indians is using NGOs to come face-to-face with India's poorer and working classes and to plant the idea of secular rights and liberties across these communities.

   D : And while it is still early days here, this trend carries a great deal of promise, especially when we consider that the growth of such NGOs has been enabled by a middle class with an active interest in political reforms.

   E : This bottom-up civil consciousness, non-political and non-partisan as it is, is a sign of a new kind of democracy in India.

The correct sequence should be

(a) BDEAC   (b) AEBDC

(c) CDABE   (d) EBADC   *[MAT, 2016]*

3. A : Over the last few decades, green tea has undergone many scientific and medical studies to determine the extent of its long health benefits.

   B : In China, there is a proverb - "Better to be deprived of food for three days, than tea of one"– and they were using the tea as a cure for headache, depression and many other ailments.

   C : But it's true that Chinese people were well aware about green tea from ancient time.

   D : We came to know about this green tea very late.

   E : If I had said that tea is a healthy drink some years before the introduction of green tea, I might have been ridiculed.

The correct sequence should be

(a) EDCBA   (b) CDBAE

(c) EBDAC   (d) DECAB   *[MAT, 2011]*

4. A : Basically, we analysed the companies that got listed in the calendar year 2007 and calculated their averages for subscription, listing gains, funds raised and the valuations at which they hit the market.

B : This was to ascertain whether promoters are being cautious and relying on other sources to grow their business or they are back to the primary market.

C : We also took a close look into whether new businesses are growing or are the safe harbours, such as infotech, construction and power, approaching the market again.

D : We compared them with the companies that hit the primary market after the market recovery during the period January 2009-March 2010.

E : We analysed the IPOs listed in 2007 and those in 2009-10 to figure out how the approach has changed after the market mayhem of 2008-09.

The correct sequence should be

(a) EBCAD   (b) DBECA

(c) CBADE   (d) ABCDE   *[MAT, 2010]*

5. A : Many so-called indicators for stocks and indexes take on complex hues, such as taking on moving averages of moving averages and so on.

B : A moving-average-based indicator will always be a little late, and you should naturally be suspicious of any 'formula' that can predict the next move, based purely on moving averages of price.

C : The moving average is simply a 'smoothing' function– it gets rid of periodic volatility to tell you the recent trend.

D : At best, they can tell you a trend and if the hypothesis is that the trend will sustain, and that bears out historically in enough instances, you might have a hope with it.

E : But smoothing has its disadvantages; it reacts slowly to sudden changes, so it will only tell you that the trend has changed after the trend has changed, sometimes too late to actually take action.

The correct sequence should be

(a) ABCDE   (b) DBCAE

(c) ACEBD   (d) BECAD   *[MAT, 2011]*

6. A : The people in the city were living in an environment where the front end of private goods had largely fallen into place, while the support infrastructure at the back end– transport, water, power– was in shambles, full of ominous creaks and missing pieces.

B : The consuming class noticed that they could buy a house, but they didn't have sewage or water connections or garbage disposal systems.

C : In the cities, the rise of the middle class (who for the first time in India were educated as well as increasingly wealthy, engaged consumers) helped sharpen the focus on India's hopelessly dilapidated urban infrastructure.

D : But it is only since the late 1990s that the popular demand for better infrastructure became more strident.

E : If they bought a car, they had to drive it on terrible roads and if they chose to walk, they found they could easily fall into an open storm drain or a random hole in the sidewalk that had been gouged open to lay pipes and then forgotten.

The correct sequence should be

(a) DCBEA   (b) BADCE

(c) EDBAC   (d) BDECA   *[MAT, 2016]*

7. A : The Plant in Mexico will have an annual capacity of 26300 tonnes of plastic films and the one in Egypt will have 77000 tonnes.

B : While the cost for setting up, the Mexico plant is $ 110 million, the company had spent $ 135 million on the Egyptian plant.

C : The new plants have been set up as part of $ 250 million (around ₹ 1250 crore) investment plans announced last year.

D : Flexible packaging major Uflex on Sunday said it will operationalise two new facilities in Egypt and Mexico by June to grow its footprint in the overseas markets.

E : "The Mexican facility, which is the second Uflex plant in that country will be inaugurated on 16th May and we will follow it up with the Egyptian plant in June", Flex Group Chairman and MD said.

The correct sequence should be

(a) BDACE   (b) DCBEA

(c) AEBCD   (d) CABDE   *[MAT, 2010]*

8. A : This is an exciting time to be working in India as the entertainment market is evolving rapidly and astutely, representing an enormous opportunity.

B : A lot has changed in these years both in terms of our growth in India, the business environment and also the way the economy is growing.

C : The Indian market presents a tremendous opportunity for us to build a relevant and engaging family entertainment brand for the audience.

D : But what hasn't changed is Disney's vision to build a family entertainment brand in the country.

E : Even though, we have been here as a company for just over five years, Disney stories and products have enthralled India families and kids for decades.

The correct sequence should be

(a) DABCE   (b) ABEDC

(c) CEBDA   (d) EABCD   *[MAT, 2010]*

9. A : It has a reach that caters million of homes, but it is now seeing. South in a 'more specific' way as 5000 of the 10000 theatres of the country are located in this region.

B : It has been more than five years since the $ 36 billion global media and entertainment conglomerate stepped into India, where it has invested $ 0.5 billion and has 100 licensees.

C : Say Walt Disney and it immediately conjures up myriad cartoon characters that are popular all over the world.

D : But operating in a market that has diversity as its foundation, Walt Disney seeks to carve a new identity– Indian Walt Disney.

E : Outside of the US, India is one of the largest markets where Disney has invested in for local production.

The correct sequence should be

(a) AEDBC   (b) EDCBA

(c) DCABE   (d) CBDEA   *[MAT, 2010]*

10. A : The upsurge of public activism against the setting up of Special Economic Zones, which eventually forced the State Government to announce the scrapping of all 15 such projects, is an impressive case in point.

B : Early last year, a similar agitation coerced the government into calling for a revision of the Goa-Regional Plan 2011, a controversial document that opened up large swathes of land, including green belts and coastal stretches, for construction.

C : The broad-based agitation against SEZs has demonstrated the power of popular protest in the State.

D : Those opposed to the projects had questioned the prosperity of the government acquiring large tracts of land and then selling them to promoters at low prices.

E : A coastal State with an area of 3700 square kilometers and a population of about 1.4 million, Goa has always been extremely sensitive to the impact of unrestrained economic development.

The correct sequence should be

(a) BCDEA   (b) CDEAB
(c) EABCD   (d) DABCE   *[MAT, 2010]*

Exercise 7

1. A : But I always felt somewhere in my mind that I loved acting.

B : He never wanted me to be an actor, as he didn't look upon theatre or acting as respectable vocation.

C : Firstly, there was no tradition of theatre in my family.

D : I am talking specifically of acting, not theatre in general.

E : My parents were old- fashioned.

F : I will answer all your queries a little elaborately.

G : Let alone theatre, arts in general had no place of respect in my family.

H : My father was a government servant.   **[SBI (PO), 2007]**

(i) Which of the following will be the LAST (EIGHTH) sentence?
   (a) G   (b) C   (c) H   (d) D   (e) E

(ii) Which of the following will be the FIRST sentence?
   (a) A   (b) B   (c) D   (d) C   (e) F

(iii) Which of the following will be the SIXTH sentence?
   (a) B   (b) C   (c) A   (d) D   (e) E

(iv) Which of the following will be the FOURTH sentence?
   (a) D   (b) E   (c) A   (d) B   (e) G

(v) Which of the following will be the THIRD sentence?
   (a) H   (b) E   (c) G   (d) C   (e) A

2. A : Thus, if we really value it, we will work hard to make it a reality.

B : Inner peace is the most exclusive thing that a human being can seek.

C : The most important criterion in order to experience it is to value the importance of inner peace.

D : To experience inner peace one doesn't have to retreat to a Himalayan cave; rather, one can experience inner peace seated exactly where one is by watching these thoughts.

E : Nobody can gift the other inner peace; at the same time, it is only one's own thoughts that can rob him of his inner peace.

[PNB (Specialist Officer), 2010]

(i) Which of the following should be the FIFTH sentence after rearrangement?

(a) A   (b) B   (c) C   (d) D   (e) E

(ii) Which of the following should be the FOURTH sentence after rearrangement?

(a) E   (b) D   (c) C   (d) B   (e) A

(iii) Which of the following should be the SECOND sentence after rearrangement?

(a) E   (b) D   (c) C   (d) B   (e) A

(iv) Which of the following should be the FIRST sentence after rearrangement?

(a) A   (b) B   (c) C   (d) D   (e) E

(v) Which of the following should be the THIRD sentence after rearrangement?

(a) A   (b) B   (c) C   (d) D   (e) E

3. A. Increased competition, globalisation and the need for enormous resource have nudged priorities which once held the fort.

B. In order to achieve these, hype and sensationalism is put into spice up the news, which have robbed news stories of credibility.

C. This is only possible if a lot more thought is put into the gathering and presentation of the daily news and delivering it much more sensitively to its receivers/users.

D. Technological innovation and economic change have transformed the news industry to the extent where its original definition as a public service no longer holds good.

E. In order to win it back, the media should make full use of the tremendous power that the democracy blesses it with.

F. These included public good and social responsibility. But sadly, today, these have made way for a business target of commercial viability and a chase of viewership.

[Oriental Bank of Commerce (PO), 2010]

(i) Which of the following sentence should be the SIXTH (LAST) after rearrangement?

    (a) A   (b) B   (c) C   (d) D   (e) F

(ii) Which of the following sentence should be the THIRD after rearrangement?

    (a) A   (b) E   (c) D   (d) F   (e) C

(iii) Which of the following sentence should be the FIFTH after rearrangement ?

    (a) A   (b) B   (c) E   (d) C   (e) F

(iv) Which of the following sentence should be the FIRST after rearrangement?

    (a) A   (b) B   (c) C   (d) D   (e) E

(v) Which of the following sentence should be the SECOND after rearrangement?

    (a) A   (b) B   (c) D   (d) E   (e) F

4. A : It governs all other powers, physical, mental, etc.

B : The mobility of the purpose helps your thoughts to break all the boundaries.

C : The power of mind is enormous.

D : Therefore, to achieve it, one should try to kindle the mind power.

E : When thoughts transcend limitations, the goal is reachable.

F : The pre-requisite is that your mind should be inspired by some good purpose.

[RBI (Grade B), 2008]

(i) Which of the following should be the SECOND sentence after rearrangement?

    (a) A   (b) B   (c) C   (d) D   (e) E

(ii) Which of the following should be the FIRST sentence after rearrangement?

    (a) A   (b) B   (c) C   (d) D   (e) E

(iii) Which of the following should be the SIXTH (LAST) sentence
after rearrangement?

    (a) A   (b) B   (c) C   (d) D   (e) E

(iv) Which of the following should be the FOURTH sentence after
rearrangement?

    (a) A   (b) B   (c) C   (d) D   (e) E

(v) Which of the following should be the FIFTH sentence after
rearrangement?

    (a) A   (b) B   (c) C   (d) D   (e) E

5. A : In all varieties of humour, especially the subtle ones it is
therefore what the reader thinks which gives extra meaning to
these verses.

B : But such a verse may also be enjoyed at the surface level.

C : Nonsense verse is not of the most sophisticated forms of
literature.

D : This fulfils the author's main intention in such a verse which is
to give pleasure.

E : However, the reader who understands the broad implications
of the content and allusion finds greater pleasure.

F : The reason being it requires the reader to supply a meaning
beyond the surface meaning.   **[Canara Bank (PO), 2009]**

(i) Which of the following is the FIFTH sentence?

    (a) D   (b) E   (c) B   (d) C   (e) A

(ii) Which of the following is the SIXTH (LAST) sentence?

    (a) F   (b) E   (c) D   (d) A   (e) C

(iii) Which of the following is the FIRST sentence?

    (a) E   (b) A   (c) F   (d) D   (e) C

(iv) Which of the following is the SECOND sentence?

    (a) A   (b) E   (c) F   (d) B   (e) C

(v) Which of the following is the THIRD sentence?

    (a) A   (b) B   (c) F   (d) C   (e) D

6. A : Expansion of retail banking especially has a lot of scope , since
retail assets are just 22% of the total banking assets.

B : Where they do not find it viable to open branches they may
open satellite offices in these areas.

C : There is tremendous scope for the expansion of banking in India.

D : Banks can also diversify beyond cities to semi urban and rural areas.

E : In these ways, a transition from class banking to mass banking can take place.

F : They can also collaborate with local stakeholders in order to extend microcredit services to those living there.

[PNB (Agriculture Officer), 2009]

(i) Which of the following should be the THIRD sentence after rearrangement?

(a) B   (b) C   (c) D   (d) E   (e) F

(ii) Which of the following should be the FIRST sentence after rearrangement?

(a) A   (b) B   (c) C   (d) D   (e) E

(iii) Which of the following should be the FIFTH sentence after rearrangement?

(a) B   (b) C   (c) D   (d) E   (e) F

(iv) Which of the following should be the SIXTH (LAST) sentence after rearrangement?

(a) A   (b) B   (c) C   (d) D   (e) E

(v) Which of the following should be the SECOND sentence after rearrangement?

(a) A   (b) B   (c) C   (d) D   (e) E

7. A : The able bodied men of the tribe gathered to discuss how to climb the mountain.

B : As part of their plundering they kidnapped a baby of one of the families.

C : One day, the mountain tribe invaded those living in the valley.

D : "We couldn't climb the mountain. How could you?", they asked. "It wasn't your baby!" she replied.

E : There were two tribes in the Andes-one lived in the valley and the other high up in the mountains.

F : Two days later, they noticed the child's mother coming down the mountain that they hadn't yet figured out how to climb.

[SBI (Clerk), 2008]

(i) Which of the following should be the SECOND sentence after rearrangement?

(a) A   (b) B   (c) C   (d) D   (e) E

(ii) Which of the following should be the FIFTH sentence after rearrangement?

   (a) F   (b) E   (c) D   (d) C   (e) B

(iii) Which of the following should be the FIRST sentence after rearrangement?

   (a) A   (b) B   (c) C   (d) D   (e) E

(iv) Which of the following should be the SIXTH (LAST) sentence after rearrangement?

   (a) A   (b) B   (c) C   (d) D   (e) E

(v) Which of the following should be the THIRD sentence after rearrangement?

   (a) A   (b) B   (c) C   (d) D   (e) E

8. A : The sailor was told it was placed there as a warning signal to sailors to warn them of danger.

B : He returned to the spot a few years later as captain of his own ship.

C : The ship was at sea for many days and finally anchored near the coastline.

D : The night was stormy and without a warning signal his ship was wrecked on that very rock.

E : One of the sailors on board saw a bell tied to a dangerous submerged rock.

F : As a joke the sailor decided to steal the bell and hide it despite being informed of this.   **[SBI (Clerk), 2008]**

(i) Which of the following should be the FIRST sentence after rearrangement?

   (a) A   (b) B   (c) C   (d) D   (e) E

(ii) Which of the following should be the SECOND sentence after rearrangement?

   (a) A   (b) B   (c) C   (d) D   (e) E

(iii) Which of the following should be the THIRD sentence after rearrangement?

   (a) A   (b) B   (c) C   (d) D   (e) E

(iv) Which of the following should be the FIFTH sentence after rearrangement?

   (a) A   (b) B   (c) C   (d) D   (e) E

(v) Which of the following should be the SIXTH (LAST) sentence after rearrangement?

(a) A   (b) B   (c) C   (d) D   (e) E

9. A : The blame for lacking creativity is, however, put on the present generation by the modern educationists.

B : The concept of homework began so that the pupils could revise that was being taught in the class.

C : By doing so, most of the schools took away the leisure time of the children.

D : Instead, these educationists should suggest lowering of burden of homework to the commission for educational reforms.

E : The purpose of this concept was, however, defeated when the schools started overburdening students with so called homework.

F : Lack of such leisure time does not allow the children to develop creative pursuits.   *[Corporation Bank (PO), 2009]*

(i) Which of the following sentence should be the THIRD after rearrangement?

(a) A   (b) E   (c) D   (d) F   (e) C

(ii) Which of the following sentence should be the FIRST after rearrangement?

(a) A   (b) B   (c) C   (d) D   (e) E

(iii) Which of the following sentence should be the SECOND after rearrangement?

(a) A   (b) B   (c) D   (d) E   (e) F

(iv) Which of the following sentence should be the SIXTH (LAST) after rearrangement?

(a) B   (b) C   (c) D   (d) E   (e) F

(v) Which of the following sentence should be the FIFTH after rearrangement?

(a) A   (b) B   (c) C   (d) E   (e) F

10. A : Had it been not for them, Indian banks would have had their hands tied down too.

B : Today, almost all the countries are facing the heat of recession.

C : One of these is the strict RBI and SEBI rules which regulated banking sector very efficiently.

D : This could have led to massive losses to them, which could have percolated to other sectors as well.

E : However, there are a few things which help India in bouncing back from the state of recession.

F : Like others India too has not remained immune to the epidemic. **[Andhra Bank (PO), 2009]**

(i) Which of the following sentence should be the THIRD after rearrangement?

(a) A   (b) E   (c) D   (d) F   (e) C

(ii) Which of the following sentence should be the FIRST after rearrangement?

(a) A   (b) B   (c) C   (d) D   (e) E

(iii) Which of the following sentence should be the SECOND after rearrangement?

(a) A   (b) B   (c) D   (d) E   (e) F

(iv) Which of the following sentence should be the SIXTH (LAST) after rearrangement?

(a) C   (b) E   (c) D   (d) B   (e) F

(v) Which of the following sentence should be the FIFTH after rearrangement?

(a) B   (b) C   (c) A   (d) E   (e) F

Exercise 8

1. A : When these millennium development goals were first formulated in 1990, 53.5% of all Indian children were malnourished.

B : This would still be below the target of reducing malnourishment to 28.6%.

C : India has been moderately successful in reducing poverty.

D : Since then, progress has been slow.

E : Today, it is estimated that malnourishment could decline to 40% by the end of 2015.

F : However, eradicating hunger alongwith malnourishment still remains a key challenge, according to the millennium development goals. **[IBPS (PO), 2015]**

(i) Which of the following should be the FOURTH sentence after rearrangement?

(a) A   (b) B   (c) C   (d) E   (e) D

(ii) Which of the following should be the THIRD sentence after rearrangement?

(a) A   (b) B   (c) F   (d) D   (e) E

(iii) Which of the following should be the SECOND sentence after rearrangement?

(a) A   (b) B   (c) C   (d) D   (e) F

(iv) Which of the following should be the FIRST sentence after rearrangement?

(a) A   (b) B   (c) C   (d) D   (e) E

(v) Which of the following should be the LAST (SIXTH) sentence after rearrangement?

(a) A   (b) F   (c) D   (d) C   (e) B

2. A : So while these partnerships are at times messy and controversial, on balance, they are a force for good.

B : NGOs help companies reach and meet the needs of parts of the market that companies do not understand such as the marginalised, where NGOs have unique insight.

C : But before concluding that such partnership are valueless it is worth recalling the reasons why they took off in the first place.

D : For NGOs too, partnerships with firms have their uses, with companies providing money and ways of influencing the minds and behaviour of millions of people.

E : There are many opponents to the close ties between companies and charities Non-Governmental Organisations (NGOs).

F : NGOs are also better than companies at attracting and retaining idealistic talent, who sometimes end up even being absorbed by the companies to administer the policies they had advocated when they worked for NGOs.   *[IBPS RRB, 2015]*

(i) Which of the following should be the SECOND sentence after the rearrangement?

(a) A   (b) B   (c) C   (d) D   (e) E

(ii) Which of the following should be the SIXTH (LAST) sentence after the rearrangement?

(a) A   (b) B   (c) C   (d) D   (e) F

(iii) Which of the following should be the FIFTH sentence after the rearrangement?

(a) A   (b) B   (c) C   (d) D   (e) E

(iv) Which of the following should be the THIRD sentence after the rearrangement?

(a) A   (b) B   (c) D   (d) E   (e) F

(v) Which of the following should be the FIRST sentence after the rearrangement?

(a) A   (b) B   (c) D   (d) E   (e) F

3. A : Take e.g. the market for learning dancing.

B : This could never happen if there was a central board of dancing education which enforced strict standards of what will be taught and how such things are to be taught.

C : The Indian education system is built on the presumption that if something is good for one child, it is good for all children.

D : More importantly, different teachers and institutes have developed different ways of teaching dancing.

E : There are very different dance forms that attract students with different tastes.

F : If however, we can effectively decentralise education and if the government did not obsessively control what would be the 'syllabus' and what will be the method of instruction, there could be an explosion of new and innovative courses geared towards serving various riches of learners.

[SBI (PO), 2015]

(i) Which of the following should be the LAST (SIXTH) sentence after the rearrangement?

(a) A   (b) F   (c) D   (d) C   (e) B

(ii) Which of the following should be the THIRD sentence after the rearrangement?

(a) A   (b) B   (c) F   (d) D   (e) E

(iii) Which of the following should be the SECOND sentence after the rearrangement?

(a) A   (b) B   (c) C   (d) D   (e) F

(iv) Which of the following should be the FIRST sentence after the rearrangement?

(a) A   (b) B   (c) C   (d) D   (e) E

(v) Which of the following should be the FOURTH sentence after the rearrangement?

(a) A   (b) B   (c) C   (d) E   (e) D

4. A : Now when the wise sage returned he saw a large crowd gathered on the road and his well-fed disciple in its midst, accepting offerings for the rock.

B : "Look!", they exclaimed in excitement, "There is something written on the rock! What can it mean?"

C : The sage was away and his disciple, who loved to put on an air of learning, examined the drawings on the rock and proclaimed, "Each person using the road must worship the rock and make an offering. The one who ignores this will turn into a donkey!"

D : He examined the rock, moved it aside, lifted out a port of gold hidden beneath it which he said had to be used to keep the road in good repair and kept his disciple cleaning cowsheds for the remainder of the year alone for his greed.

E : A large crowd gathered and they all had the same question so they decided to go to the ashram of a wise sage.

F : The road was a very busy one which connected a large number of villages and one day a group of students discovered a rock.

[SBI (Clerk), 2015]

(i) Which of the following should be the FIFTH sentence after the rearrangement?

(a) A   (b) C   (c) D   (d) E   (e) F

(ii) Which of the following should be the SECOND sentence after the rearrangement?

(a) A   (b) B   (c) C   (d) D   (e) F

(iii) Which of the following should be the SIXTH (LAST) sentence after the rearrangement?

(a) A   (b) B   (c) C   (d) D   (e) F

(iv) Which of the following should be the FIRST sentence after the rearrangement?

(a) A   (b) B   (c) D   (d) E   (e) F

(v) Which of the following should be the THIRD sentence after the rearrangement?

(a) A   (b) B   (c) D   (d) E   (e) F

5. A : Basic human needs also include a sense of belongingness, a feeling of control over one's life.

B : Motivation and inspiration energise people into action.

C : Ability to live up to one's ideals besides all these is also a fundamental need.

D : This is done not by pushing them in the right direction as control mechanisms.

E : Such feelings touch us deeply and elicit powerful response.

F : But it is done by satisfying basic human needs for achievement.

[SBI (Clerk), 2015]

(i) Which of the following should be the FIFTH sentence after rearrangement?

   (a) A   (b) C   (c) D   (d) E   (e) B

(ii) Which of the following should be the SECOND sentence after rearrangement?

   (a) A   (b) B   (c) C   (d) D   (e) F

(iii) Which of the following should be the SIXTH (LAST) sentence after rearrangement?

   (a) A   (b) B   (c) C   (d) D   (e) E

(iv) Which of the following should be the FIRST sentence after rearrangement?

   (a) A   (b) B   (c) D   (d) E   (e) C

(v) Which of the following should be the FOURTH sentence after rearrangement?

   (a) A   (b) B   (c) D   (d) E   (e) C

6. A : Beena grew day by day and was charming and polite but as the goddess predicted she had to have a new outfit every day and for a while the king and queen were happy to let her have her way but soon realised that this had to stop.

B : They longed for the child and prayed till finally one day their prayers were heard but the goddess warned, you will soon have a little girl and though she will be a loving child, she will love new clothes too much and will be cursed if she coverts, another's clothes.

C : They tried to get her mend her ways but in vain and one day when Beena saw a beautiful girl simply dressed in cotton sari and noticed how people were admiring the simply dressed girl she demanded the dress.

D : The kingdom was at peace, subjects were happy and there was a bumper crop but the king and queen were very sad.

E : As foretold, Beena turned into an onion. A plant with many layers to symbolise the many dresses she had.

F : The king and queen were ready to accept this flow and when the queen gave birth to a baby girl the entire kingdom rejoiced. **[SBI (Clerk), 2015]**

(i) Which of the following should be the FIFTH sentence after the rearrangement?

(a) A   (b) C   (c) D   (d) E   (e) F

(ii) Which of the following should be the SIXTH (LAST) sentence after the rearrangement?

(a) A   (b) B   (c) C   (d) D   (e) E

(iii) Which of the following should be the FIRST sentence after the rearrangement?

(a) A   (b) B   (c) C   (d) D   (e) F

(iv) Which of the following should be the SECOND sentence after the rearrangement?

(a) A   (b) B   (c) C   (d) D   (e) F

(v) Which of the following should be the THIRD sentence after the rearrangement?

(a) A   (b) B   (c) D   (d) E   (e) F

7. So how is global competition changing companies?

A : For example, a group with a Europe-wide pay freeze may have to be flexible enough to authorise salary increase to specialists and managers in developing countries who are still able to jump ship for a better offer.

B : Second with emerging market companies as well as established multinationals as rivals there is no way these can be igonored.

C : First businesses are having to respond faster than before to pay changes.

D : A case in point today is Africa where rapid growth in key countries notably Nigeria has persuaded many business people that the continent's time may finally have arrived.

E : The sight of well-paid expatriate foreign managers inspire these local Indian executives to ask for more and employers have to respond.

F : So, such countries where people move easily-like India are seeing executive pay rising rapidly. **[IBPS (PO), 2014]**

(i) Which of the following should be the SIXTH (LAST) sentence after the rearrangement?

    (a) F   (b) E   (c) D   (d) C   (e) B

(ii) Which of the following should be the FOURTH sentence after the rearrangement?

    (a) A   (b) B   (c) C   (d) D   (e) F

(iii) Which of the following should be the FIFTH sentence after the rearrangement?

    (a) A   (b) B   (c) C   (d) E   (e) F

(iv) Which of the following should be the SECOND sentence after the rearrangement?

    (a) A   (b) B   (c) C   (d) E   (e) F

(v) Which of the following should be the THIRD sentence after the rearrangement?

    (a) A   (b) B   (c) C   (d) D   (e) E

8. A : But it is normal for rates to vary somewhat.

    B : The rate at which these actions emerge is sometimes a worry for parents.

    C : As a child grows, his or her nervous system becomes more mature.

    D : Having said that variation is normal, nearly all children begin to exhibit certain motor skills at a fairly consistent rate unless-some type of disability is present.

    E : As this happens, the child becomes more and more capable of performing increasingly complex actions.

    F : Hence, they frequently fret about whether or not their children are developing these skills at a normal rate.   *[SBI (PO), 2014]*

(i) Which of the following should be the THIRD sentence after the rearrangement?

    (a) A   (b) B   (c) C   (d) E   (e) F

(ii) Which of the following should be the SIXTH (LAST) sentence after the rearrangement?

    (a) A   (b) B   (c) C   (d) D   (e) E

(iii) Which of the following should be the FIRST sentence after the rearrangement?

    (a) A   (b) B   (c) C   (d) D   (e) E

(iv) Which of the following should be the SECOND sentence after the rearrangement?

(a) A   (b) B   (c) F   (d) D   (e) E

(v) Which of the following should be the FOURTH sentence after the rearrangement?

(a) A   (b) D   (c) B   (d) F   (e) E

9. A : All the labourers and the soldiers turned around and saw a hut just a few steps away from the palace gate.

B : Then suddenly his eyes fell on something and he shouted, "What is that? I did not see that before."

C : Before inviting the King to see the palace, the minister decided to take a final look "Splended!" the minister exclaimed, looking at the palace.

D : Many labourers were put to work and in a few days the palace was ready.

E : Once, Veer decided to build a palace on a river bank and ordered his ministers to survey the site and start the construction.

F : King Veer was known for his justice and kindness in whose kingdom, everyone was leading a happy and content life and his people loved him and were proud of him.   **[SBI (Clerk), 2014]**

(i) Which of the following sentences should be the FIRST sentence after rearrangement?

(a) A   (b) B   (c) C   (d) D   (e) F

(ii) Which of the following sentences should be the SECOND sentence after rearrangement?

(a) A   (b) B   (c) C   (d) D   (e) E

(iii) Which of the following sentence should be the FOURTH sentence after rearrangement?

(a) A   (b) B   (c) C   (d) D   (e) E

(iv) Which of the following sentences should be the THIRD sentence after rearrangement?

(a) A   (b) B   (c) C   (d) D   (e) E

(v) Which of the following sentences should be the LAST sentence after rearrangement?

(a) A   (b) B   (c) C   (d) D   (e) E

10. A : He did whatever work was assigned to him and soon the lion became so fond of him that he promised to give him a cart full of almonds as pension when he (the squirrel) retired.

B : Once a squirrel joined the service of the king of the forest, the lion.

C : The squirrel had waited so long for this day but when he saw the almonds, he was seized with sadness as he realised that they were of no use to him now when he had lost all his teeth.

D : However, he envied other squirrels in the forest because of their carefree life which he could not enjoy as he had to be by the king's side all the time.

E : He consoled himself with the thought that at the end of his career, he would receive cart full of almonds, a food that only a few squirrels got to taste in their lifetime.

F : Finally, the day came when it was time for him to retire and as promised the king gave a grand banquet in his honour and presented him with a cart full of almonds.

[SBI (Clerk), 2014]

(i) Which of the following should be the SECOND sentence after the rearrangement?

(a) A   (b) B   (c) F   (d) D   (e) E

(ii) Which of the following should be the FIRST sentence after the rearrangement?

(a) A   (b) C   (c) B   (d) D   (e) E

(iii) Which of the following should be the FIFTH sentence after the rearrangement?

(a) E   (b) D   (c) B   (d) F   (e) A

(iv) Which of the following should be the FOURTH sentence after the rearrangement?

(a) A   (b) B   (c) C   (d) F   (e) E

(v) Which of the following should be the SIXTH (LAST) sentence after the rearrangement?

(a) C   (b) D   (c) A   (d) B   (e) E

Exercise 9

1. A : The group desired to enhance the learning experience in schools with an interactive digital medium that could be used within and outside the classroom.

   B : Then the teacher can act on the downloaded data rather than collect it from each and every student and thereby save his time and effort.

   C : Edutor, decided the group of engineers, all alumni of the Indian Institute of Technology, when they founded Edutor Technologies in August, 2009.

   D : They can even take tests and submit them digitally using the same tablets and the teacher in turn can download the tests using the company's cloud services.

   E : With this desire they created a solution that digitises school textbooks and other learning material so that students no longer need to carry as many books to school and back as before, but can access their study material on their touch-screen tablets.

   F : A mechanic works on motors and an accountant has his computer. Likewise, if a student has to work on a machine of device, what should it be called? **[SBI (PO), 2013]**

   (i) Which of the following sentences should be the FIRST after rearrangement?

   (a) F (b) D (c) A (d) C (e) E

   (ii) Which of the following sentences should be the THIRD after rearrangement?

   (a) A (b) B (c) D (d) E (e) F

   (iii) Which of the following sentences should be the SIXTH (LAST) after rearrangement?

   (a) A (b) F (c) E (d) B (e) D

   (iv) Which of the following sentences should be the FOURTH after rearrangement?

   (a) A (b) F (c) E (d) B (e) C

   (v) Which of the following sentences should be the FIFTH after rearrangement?

   (a) A (b) D (c) C (d) E (e) F

2. A : The storm-given the name Hercules-closed major roads with
       snowdrifts.
   B : A fierce winter storm brought dangerous glacial temperature in
       New York on Friday.
   C : Weather experts said the wind chill temperature would
       plummet to – 25° in New York.
   D : With more than 24 inches of snow falling in the city, a state of
       emergency was declared.
   E : More than 4000 international and domestic flights were also
       cancelled.
   F : Indeed storms are disastrous.   *[IBPS (Clerk), 2013]*

   (i) Which of the following should be the FIRST sentence after the
       rearrangement?
       (a) E   (b) B   (c) D   (d) C   (e) F

   (ii) Which of the following should be the FOURTH sentence after the
        rearrangement?
        (a) D   (b) F   (c) B   (d) E   (e) C

   (iii) Which of the following should be the FIFTH sentence after the
         rearrangement?
         (a) E   (b) D   (c) B   (d) C   (e) F

   (iv) Which of the following should be the SIXTH (LAST) sentence after
        the rearrangement?
        (a) A   (b) D   (c) F   (d) E   (e) C

   (v) Which of the following should be the SECOND sentence after the
       rearrangement?
       (a) A   (b) D   (c) F   (d) B   (e) C

3. A : However, while reading, they would not know when to pause
       and what to emphasise.
   B : Since then, their use has been regularised and the punctuation
       rules have been followed by all.
   C : In earlier days, people learnt by reading out loud.
   D : But not everybody used the same punctuations for the same
       thing.
   E : To address this problem, various signs depicting various
       punctuations were introduced.
   F : Thus, firmer guidelines regarding punctuations were framed so
       that everyone used them in a similar way.   *[IBPS (PO), 2012]*

(i) Which of the following sentences should be the the SECOND after rearrangement?
(a) A   (b) B   (c) D   (d) E   (e) F

(ii) Which of the following sentences should be the THIRD after rearrangement?
(a) A   (b) E   (c) D   (d) F   (e) C

(iii) Which of the following sentences should be the FIFTH after rearrangement?
(a) B   (b) C   (c) A   (d) E   (e) F

(iv) Which of the following sentences should be the SIXTH (LAST) after rearrangement?
(a) C   (b) E   (c) D   (d) B   (e) F

(v) Which of the following sentences should be the FIRST after rearrangement?
(a) A   (b) B   (c) C   (d) D   (e) E

4. A : The policy makers in most of the developing economies recognise this importance and have been implementing a host of programmes and measures to achieve rural development objectives.

B : While some of these countries have achieved impressive results from those programmes and measures, others have failed to make a significant dent in the problem of persistent rural underdevelopment.

C : The socio-economic disparities between rural and urban areas are widening and creating tremendous pressure on the social and economic fabric of many such developing economies.

D : These factors, among many others, tend to highlight the importance of rural development.

E : Although, millions of rural people have escaped poverty as a result of rural development in many Asian countries, a large majority of rural people continue to suffer from persistent poverty.   *[IBPS (PO), 2012]*

(i) Which of the following should be the THIRD sentence after rearrangement?
(a) A   (b) B   (c) C   (d) D   (e) E

(ii) Which of the following should be the LAST (FIFTH) sentence after rearrangement?
(a) A   (b) B   (c) C   (d) D   (e) E

(iii) Which of the following should be the FOURTH sentence after rearrangement?

(a) C   (b) B   (c) A   (d) D   (e) E

(iv) Which of the following should be the FIRST sentence after rearrangement?

(a) A   (b) B   (c) C   (d) D   (e) E

(v) Which of the following should be the SECOND sentence after rearrangement?

(a) D   (b) E   (c) C   (d) B   (e) A

5. A : It is no wonder that a majority of these excluded and low achievers come from the most deprived sections of the society.

   B : They are precisely those who are supposed to be empowered through education.

   C : With heightened political consciousness about the plight of these to be empowered people, never in the history of India has the demand for inclusive education been as fervent as today.

   D : They either never enroll or they drop out of schools at different stages during these 8 years.

   E : Of the nearly 200 million children in the age group between 6 and 14 years, more than half do not complete 8 years of elementary education.

   F : Of those who do complete 8 years of schooling the achievement levels of a large percentage, in language and mathematics, is unacceptably low. *[IBPS (Specialist Officer), 2012]*

(i) Which of the following should be the THIRD sentence after rearrangement?

(a) A   (b) B   (c) C   (d) D   (e) F

(ii) Which of the following should be the FIRST sentence after rearrangement?

(a) A   (b) B   (c) C   (d) D   (e) E

(iii) Which of the following should be the SECOND sentence after rearrangement?

(a) F   (b) E   (c) D   (d) C   (e) B

(iv) Which of the following should be the FOURTH sentence after rearrangement?

(a) A   (b) B   (c) C   (d) D   (e) E

(v) Which of the following should be the FIFTH sentence after rearrangement?

(a) F   (b) E   (c) D   (d) B   (e) A

6. A : If China is the world's factory, India has become the world's outsourcing centre–keeping in line with this image.

B : But India's future depends crucially on its ability to compete fully in the Creative Economy–not just in tech and software, but across design and entrepreneurship; arts, culture and entertainment; and the knowledge-based professions of medicine, finance and law.

C : While its creative assets outstrip those of other emerging competitors, India must address several challenges to increase its international competitiveness as the world is in the midst of a sweeping transformation.

D : This transformation is evident in the fact that the world is moving from an industrial economy to a Creative Economy that generates wealth by harnessing intellectual labour, intangible goods and human creative capabilities.

E : Its software industry is the world's second-largest, its tech outsourcing accounts for more than half of the $ 300 billion global industry, according to a technology expert.

F : If the meeting of world leaders at Davos is any indication, India is rapidly becoming an economic 'rock star'.   *[IBPS (PO), 2012]*

(i) Which of the following should be the SIXTH (LAST) sentence after the rearrangement?

(a) A   (b) B   (c) C   (d) D   (e) E

(ii) Which of the following should be the THIRD sentence after the rearrangement?

(a) A   (b) B   (c) C   (d) D   (e) E

(iii) Which of the following should be the FIFTH sentence after the rearrangement?

(a) A   (b) B   (c) C   (d) F   (e) E

(iv) Which of the following should be the FIRST sentence after the rearrangement?

(a) F   (b) B   (c) C   (d) A   (e) E

(v) Which of the following should be the SECOND sentence after the rearrangement?

(a) A   (b) B   (c) C   (d) D   (e) F

7. A : During the examination, the invigilator noticed the chits and despite Rajesh's plea for innocence asked him to leave the examination hall.

B : At this point, Ravish realised his mistake and felt guilty, so he immediately confessed his misdeed to the invigilator and left the examination hall;

C : Rajesh forgave Ravish because Ravish had not only accepted his mistake on time, but also had not let Rajesh be punished for the wrong reason.

D : Ravish and Rajesh were in college and had been friends since childhood. However, Ravish did not trust Rajesh.

E : Another student-Satish-who had seen Ravish hiding something in Rajesh's desk stood up and informed the invigilator of what he had seen.

F : One day, Ravish decided to test Rajesh's friendship and so during one of the college examinations Ravish went early to class and hid some chits in Rajesh's desk.

G : Rajesh did not believe Satish, instead was furious that Satish has falsely blamed his friend and agreed that he would leave his examination only if Ravish was kept out of the matter.

H : After the examination was over Ravish apologised to Rajesh and promised that he would be a good friend from then onwards. *[SBI (Clerk), 2012]*

(i) Which of the following should be the FIFTH sentence after the rearrangement?

(a) G   (b) H   (c) E   (d) D   (e) C

(ii) Which of the following should be the FOURTH sentence after the rearrangement?

(a) C   (b) D   (c) E   (d) F   (e) G

(iii) Which of the following should be the EIGHTH (LAST) sentence after the rearrangement?

(a) A   (b) B   (c) C   (d) D   (e) E

(iv) Which of the following should be the FIRST sentence after the rearrangement?

(a) A   (b) B   (c) C   (d) D   (e) F

(v) Which of the following should be the SECOND sentence after the rearrangement?

(a) A   (b) B   (c) G   (d) F   (e) E

8. A : Both Ram and Sham realised their mistake and were ashamed about what they had said.

   B : Vivek happened to overhear their conversation and was very angry with both of them for criticising the tree.

   C : Two friends, Ram and Sham, were seeking respite from the searing heat of the midday sun when they saw a huge leafy tree.

   D : "It's a plain tree," said his friend. "Don't waste your time looking for fruits. It produces neither edible fruits nor good wood. It's one of the most useless trees around."

   E : "How can you say such a thing when you're enjoying the shade of this beautiful tree at this very moment?" snapped Vivek unable to control his anger.

   F : They took shelter under the huge leafy tree and soon felt cool and refreshed.

   G : Busy belittling the tree both Ram and Sham did not notice that another person, Vivek, was lying on the other side of the tree taking shelter.

   H : "What sort of tree is this? Does it produce edible fruits?" asked Ram.   **[SBI (Clerk), 2012]**

   (i) Which of the following should be the SECOND sentence after the rearrangement?
   (a) A   (b) B   (c) E   (d) F   (e) G

   (ii) Which of the following should be the EIGHTH (LAST) sentence after the rearrangement?
   (a) A   (b) B   (c) D   (d) E   (e) F

   (iii) Which of the following should be the FIFTH sentence after the rearrangement?
   (a) D   (b) E   (c) F   (d) G   (e) H

   (iv) Which of the following should be the FIRST sentence after the rearrangement?
   (a) A   (b) B   (c) C   (d) D   (e) E

   (v) Which of the following should be the FOURTH sentence after the rearrangement?
   (a) D   (b) E   (c) F   (d) G   (e) H

9. A : To elaborate briefly on these characteristics and dimensions that the author is talking about – NRMs are general tests intended to be used to classify students by percentile for measuring either aptitude or proficiency for admissions into or placement with a programme.

B : Contrastingly, the CRM, such as a locally produced achievement test, measures absolute performance that is compared only with the learning objective, hence a perfect score is theoretically obtainable by all students who have a mastery of the pre-specified material or conversely, all student's may fail the test.

C : In most of these books, the authors classify a measurement strategy as either Norm-Referenced (NRM) or Criterion-Referenced (CRM).

D : Another author points out how the type of interpretation that an NRM offers is the relative performance of the students compared with that of all the others resulting in, ideally, a bell curve distribution.

E : Numerous books on constructing and using language tests have been written by various authors.

F : CRMs, on the other hand, are more specific, achievement or diagnostic tests intended to be used for motivating students by measuring to what per cent they have achieved mastery of the taught or learned material.

G : One of the authors clearly delineates the differences of these two types by focusing on the categories of "test characteristics" and "logistical dimensions".   **[IBPS (PO), 2011]**

(i) Which of the following should be the FIRST sentence after rearrangement?

   (a) G   (b) B   (c) C   (d) D   (e) E

(ii) Which of the following should be the SEVENTH (LAST) sentence after rearrangement?

   (a) A   (b) B   (c) C   (d) D   (e) E

(iii) Which of the following should be the FIFTH sentence after rearrangement?

   (a) A   (b) B   (c) C   (d) F   (e) E

(iv) Which of the following should be the SECOND sentence after rearrangement?

   (a) A   (b) B   (c) C   (d) D   (e) F

(v) Which of the following should be the THIRD sentence after rearrangement?

   (a) A   (b) B   (c) G   (d) D   (e) E

10. A : Building of these structures required a lot of fuel to be burnt which emits a large amount of carbon dioxide in the atmosphere.

B : The major source of carbon dioxide is power plants.

C : About 20% of carbon dioxide emitted in the atmosphere comes from burning of gasoline in the engines of vehicles.

D : Buildings, both commercial and residential, represent a larger source of global warming pollution than the cars and trucks.

E : The major cause of global warming is the emission of green house gases like carbon dioxide, methane, nitrous oxide, etc., into the atmosphere.

F : These power plants emit large amounts of carbon dioxide produced from burning of fossil fuels for the purpose of electricity generation. **[Indian Bank (PO), 2011]**

(i) Which of the following should be the SECOND sentence after rearrangement?

    (a) E   (b) D   (c) C   (d) B   (e) A

(ii) Which of the following should be the THIRD sentence after rearrangement?

    (a) A   (b) B   (c) C   (d) D   (e) F

(iii) Which of the following should be the FIRST sentence after rearrangement?

    (a) A   (b) B   (c) C   (d) D   (e) E

(iv) Which of the following should be the SIXTH (LAST) sentence after rearrangement?

    (a) A   (b) B   (c) C   (d) D   (e) E

(v) Which of the following should be the FOURTH sentence after rearrangement?

    (a) E   (b) D   (c) C   (d) B   (e) A

Exercise 10

1. A : With all the bid information being available and tracked online, corruption has been considerably reduced.

B : Today, most i.e. over 95% househlods in the city enjoy a broad band connection.

C : All city contracts are now bid for online.

D : Over twenty years ago, the city government, Central Government and the private sector made concerted effort to shift the economy to include IT.

E : As our cities continue to expand and become more complex, such a system will make governance more manageable.

F : This level of connectedness has changed not only the city's economy, but also how it is governed and how business is conducted.   *[IDBI, 2011]*

(i) Which of the following should be the FIRST sentence after rearrangement?

(a) A   (b) B   (c) C   (d) D   (e) E

(ii) Which of the following should be the SECOND sentence after rearrangement?

(a) A   (b) B   (c) C   (d) D   (e) F

(iii) Which of the following should be the THIRD sentence after rearrangement?

(a) B   (b) C   (c) D   (d) E   (e) F

(iv) Which of the following should be the FIFTH sentence after rearrangement?

(a) A   (b) B   (c) C   (d) D   (e) E

(v) Which of the following should be the LAST (SIXTH) sentence after rearrangement?

(a) B   (b) C   (c) D   (d) E   (e) F

2. A : "What a waste of my tax money!". I thought, walking past the people having free Californian Chardonnay.

B : "Speak to her", he said, "She's into books".

C : The friend who had brought me there noticed my noticing her.

D : In late 2003, I was still paying taxes in America, so it horrified me that the US Consulate was hosting a "Gallo drinking appreciation event".

E : Behind them, a pianist was playing old film tunes and a slim short woman was dancing around him.   *[Corporation Bank (PO), 2011]*

(i) Which of the following would be the FOURTH sentence?

(a) A   (b) B   (c) C   (d) D   (e) E

(ii) Which of the following would be the FIRST sentence?

(a) A   (b) B   (c) C   (d) D   (e) E

(iii) Which of the following would be the FIFTH (LAST) sentence?

(a) A   (b) B   (c) C   (d) D   (e) E

(iv) Which of the following would be the SECOND sentence?

(a) A   (b) B   (c) C   (d) D   (e) E

(v) Which of the following would be the THIRD sentence?

(a) A   (b) B   (c) C   (d) D   (e) E

3. A : No one knows their names.

B : With irrigation systems, farmers were able to raise more food with less labour.

C : The first engineers lived in the middle East, probably around 3500 BC.

D : Today's city, thus, is essentially still a place where specialists live and work.

E : Thus, an increasing number of people were relieved of agricultural chores and able to gather in cities to practise specialities.

F : However, they conceived and built the elevated irrigation canal.   *[SBI (Clerk), 2011]*

(i) Which of the following will be the FOURTH sentence after rearrangement?

(a) A   (b) B   (c) C   (d) D   (e) E

(ii) Which of the following will be the FIFTH sentence after rearrangement?

(a) A   (b) B   (c) C   (d) D   (e) E

(iii) Which of the following will be the SECOND sentence after rearrangement?

(a) A   (b) B   (c) C   (d) D   (e) E

(iv) Which of the following will be the SIXTH (LAST) sentence after rearrangement?

(a) A   (b) B   (c) C   (d) D   (e) E

(v) Which of the following will be the FIRST sentence after rearrangement?

(a) A   (b) B   (c) C   (d) D   (e) E

4. A : It is a general term used to describe over 200 individual diseases.

B : The abnormal cells grow without any control, invade through normal tissue barriers and reproduce indefinitely.

C : The word 'cancer' comes from Latin, meaning a crab.

D : These characteristics include development within any tissue of a malignant growth.

E : A tumour was called cancer because of swollen veins around the area resembling a crab's limbs.

F : These diseases progress differently over a period of time and share certain characteristics. **[Bank of Baroda (PO), 2010]**

(i) Which of the following should be the SECOND sentence after rearrangement?

   (a) A   (b) B   (c) C   (d) D   (e) E

(ii) Which of the following should be the THIRD sentence after rearrangement?

   (a) A   (b) B   (c) C   (d) D   (e) E

(iii) Which of the following should be the FOURTH sentence after rearrangement?

   (a) A   (b) B   (c) C

   (d) D   (e) None of these

(iv) Which of the following should be the FIFTH sentence after rearrangement?

   (a) A   (b) B   (c) C

   (d) D   (e) None of these

(v) Which of the following should be the SIXTH (LAST) sentence after rearrangement?

   (a) A   (b) B   (c) C

   (d) D   (e) None of these

5. A : To his surprise, a little honeybee came before his throne and said, "Of all the gifts you could give me, only one will do. I'd like the power to inflict great pain whenever I choose to".

B : I hereby give you a sharp sting. But, I am sure you will use this weapon carefully only in times of anger and strife.

C : "What an awful wish!" said great Zeus, "But I will grant it".

D : And to this day, the little honeybee dies after it stings.

E : One day, Zeus, the King of Mount Olympus, was giving out gifts to beasts, birds and insects.

F : "You will get to use it only once, for using it will cost you your life." **[SBI (Clerk), 2011]**

(i) Which of the following should be the FOURTH sentence after the rearrangement?

   (a) D   (b) F   (c) B   (d) E   (e) C

(ii) Which of the following should be the SECOND sentence after the rearrangement?

(a) A   (b) D   (c) F   (d) B   (e) E

(iii) Which of the following should be the FIRST sentence after the rearrangement?

(a) E   (b) B   (c) D   (d) C   (e) F

(iv) Which of the following should be the SIXTH (LAST) sentence after the rearrangement?

(a) A   (b) D   (c) F   (d) E   (e) C

(v) Which of the following should be the FIFTH sentence after the rearrangement?

(a) E   (b) D   (c) B   (d) C   (e) F

6. A : The merchant greedily counted his gold and said, "The purse dropped had 200 pieces of gold in it. You've already stolen more than the reward! Go away or I will tell the police".

B : The judge, looking towards the merchant said, "you stated that the purse you lost contained 200 pieces of gold. Well, that's a considerable cost. But, the purse this beggar found had only 100 pieces of gold".

C : Being an honest man, the beggar came forward and handed the purse to the merchant saying, "Here is your purse. May I have my reward now?"

D : "This purse therefore cannot be the one you lost." And, with that the judge gave the purse and all the gold to the beggar.

E : A beggar found a leather purse that someone had dropped in the marketplace. On opening it, he discovered that it contained 100 pieces of gold. Then he heard a merchant shout, "A reward! A reward! to the one who finds my leather purse".

F : "I am an honest man," said the beggar defiantly. "Let us take this matter to the court. The judge patiently listened to both sides of the story.   **[SBI (Clerk), 2011]**

(i) Which of the following should be the FIRST sentence after the rearrangement?

(a) E   (b) B   (c) D   (d) C   (e) F

(ii) Which of the following should be the FOURTH sentence after the rearrangement?

(a) D   (b) F   (c) B   (d) E   (e) C

(iii) Which of the following should be the FIFTH sentence after the rearrangement?

    (a) E   (b) D   (c) B   (d) C   (e) F

(iv) Which of the following should be the SIXTH (LAST) sentence after the rearrangement?

    (a) A   (b) D   (c) F   (d) E   (e) C

(v) Which of the following should be the SECOND sentence after the rearrangement?

    (a) A   (b) D   (c) F   (d) B   (e) C

7. A : For almost 2 months now, the struggle to cap the oil well and protect large section of the country's coastline from being devastated has been the top story in the news and the major concern of the US administration.

B : At present, though, one finds little expression of this in the discussions around the oil spill.

C : In these months, it has been realised that this is an environmental crisis of gigantic proportions and is purely man-made.

D : Oil and water do not mix, as the American are being forced to accept with the tragic oil spill from a British Petroleum oil rig in the Gulf of Mexico.

E : Whether in the long-term this will compel Americans to think again about their dependence on fossil fuels and seriously embark on the path of scaling it down and encouraging alternatives remains to be seen.   **[United Bank (PO), 2010]**

(i) Which of the following should be the FIRST sentence?

    (a) A   (b) B   (c) C   (d) D   (e) E

(ii) Which of the following should be the FIFTH sentence?

    (a) E   (b) D   (c) C   (d) B   (e) A

(iii) Which of the following should be the SECOND sentence?

    (a) E   (b) D   (c) C   (d) B   (e) A

(iv) Which of the following should be the THIRD sentence?

    (a) A   (b) B   (c) C   (d) D   (e) E

(v) Which of the following should be the FOURTH sentence?

    (a) A   (b) B   (c) C   (d) D   (e) E

Answers

Exercise 1

1. (d) **2.** (a) **3.** (c) **4.** (d) **5.** (a) **6.** (b) **7.** (c) **8.** (b) **9.** (c) **10.** (c)

Exercise 2

1. (c) **2.** (c) **3.** (a) **4.** (c) **5.** (d) **6.** (d) **7.** (b) **8.** (c) **9.** (d) **10.** (b)

Exercise 3

1. (b) **2.** (b) **3.** (b) **4.** (c) **5.** (d) **6.** (a) **7.** (b) **8.** (b) **9.** (a) **10.** (c)

Exercise 4

1. (c) **2.** (b) **3.** (d) **4.** (a) **5.** (c) **6.** (b) **7.** (b) **8.** (d) **9.** (c) **10.** (a)

Exercise 5

1. (a) **2.** (c) **3.** (c) **4.** (b) **5.** (d) **6.** (c) **7.** (b) **8.** (a) **9.** (a) **10.** (c)

Exercise 6

1. (a) **2.** (b) **3.** (a) **4.** (a) **5.** (c) **6.** (b) **7.** (b) **8.** (c) **9.** (d) **10.** (c)

Exercise 7

1. (i) (d) (ii) (e) (iii) (a) (iv) (b) (v) (c) **2.** (i) (a) (ii) (c) (iii) (a) (iv) (b) (v) (d)
3. (i) (c) (ii) (d) (iii) (c) (iv) (d) (v) (a) **4.** (i) (a) (ii) (c) (iii) (d) (iv) (b) (v) (e)
5. (i) (a) (ii) (b) (iii) (e) (iv) (c) (v) (a) **6.** (i) (c) (ii) (c) (iii) (e) (iv) (e) (v) (a)
7. (i) (c) (ii) (a) (iii) (e) (iv) (d) (v) (b) **8.** (i) (c) (ii) (e) (iii) (a) (iv) (d) (v) (b)
9. (i) (e) (ii) (b) (iii) (d) (iv) (c) (v) (a) **10.** (i) (b) (ii) (b) (iii) (e) (iv) (c) (v) (c)

Exercise 8

1. (i) (e) (ii) (a) (iii) (e) (iv) (c) (v) (e) **2.** (i) (c) (ii) (a) (iii) (d) (iv) (b) (v) (d)
3. (i) (b) (ii) (e) (iii) (a) (iv) (c) (v) (e) **4.** (i) (a) (ii) (b) (iii) (d) (iv) (e) (v) (d)
5. (i) (b) (ii) (d) (iii) (e) (iv) (b) (v) (a) **6.** (i) (b) (ii) (e) (iii) (d) (iv) (b) (v) (e)
7. (i) (c) (ii) (a) (iii) (e) (iv) (c) (v) (b) **8.** (i) (b) (ii) (a) (iii) (c) (iv) (e) (v) (b)
9. (i) (e) (ii) (e) (iii) (c) (iv) (d) (v) (a) **10.** (i) (a) (ii) (c) (iii) (d) (iv) (e) (v) (a)

Exercise 9

1. (i) (a) (ii) (a) (iii) (d) (iv) (c) (v) (b) **2.** (i) (b) (ii) (d) (iii) (d) (iv) (c) (v) (b)
3. (i) (a) (ii) (b) (iii) (e) (iv) (d) (v) (c) **4.** (i) (d) (ii) (b) (iii) (c) (iv) (e) (v) (c)
5. (i) (e) (ii) (e) (iii) (c) (iv) (a) (v) (d) **6.** (i) (d) (ii) (e) (iii) (c) (iv) (a) (v) (a)
7. (i) (a) (ii) (c) (iii) (c) (iv) (d) (v) (d) **8.** (i) (d) (ii) (a) (iii) (d) (iv) (c) (v) (a)
9. (i) (e) (ii) (b) (iii) (d) (iv) (c) (v) (c) **10.** (i) (d) (ii) (e) (iii) (e) (iv) (a) (v) (c)

Exercise 10

1. (i) (d) (ii) (b) (iii) (e) (iv) (a) (v) (d) **2.** (i) (c) (ii) (d) (iii) (b) (iv) (a) (v) (e)
3. (i) (b) (ii) (e) (iii) (a) (iv) (d) (v) (c) **4.** (i) (e) (ii) (a) (iii) (e) (iv) (d) (v) (b)
5. (i) (c) (ii) (a) (iii) (a) (iv) (b) (v) (e) **6.** (i) (a) (ii) (b) (iii) (c) (iv) (b) (v) (e)
7. (i) (d) (ii) (b) (iii) (e) (iv) (c) (v) (e)